Chitreśvara-Śiva Type Coins

Classification and Attribution

Chitreśvara-Śiva Type Coins

Classification and Attribution

Devendra Handa

Aryan Books International
New Delhi

CHITREŚVARA-ŚIVA TYPE COINS
Classification and Attribution

ISBN: 978-81-7305-659-8

First Published 2022

Published by
Aryan Books International
Pooja Apartments, 4B, Ansari Road, New Delhi-110 002 (India)
Tel.: 23287589, 23255799; Fax: 91-11-23270385
E-mail: aryanbooks@gmail.com
www.aryanbooks.com

Printed in India

Dedicated to

Dr. Mrs. Yogeshwari Shastri

&

Dr. Avinash Upadhyay

(but for whose help this study would not have been possible)

With affectionate regards

Preface

More than forty years back a big hoard of copper coins containing more than two thousand pieces of Brahmaṇyadeva (Kārttikeya-Shashṭhī/Deer) and Chitreśvara type coins was discovered from the western Himalayan hill region of Tehri-Garhwal, designated in this work as Garhwal Hoard. It was documented by the Indian Numismatic, Historical and Cultural Research Foundation (INHCRF) (earlier known as Indian Institute of Research in Numismatic Studies – IIRNS) for its archives. Except an article by Prof. Ajay Mitra Shastri published in 1984 in the *Numismatic Digest* and illustration of a few coins in my book on *Tribal Coins of Ancient India* published in 2007, this important hoard has remained unpublished till now. The card indices of the hoard prepared under Prof. Shastri's supervision were handed over to me in 2004 by Mrs. Shastri as Prof. Shastri, because of his other preoccupations, could not complete the study of this important hoard till his sudden and untimely demise in 2002. These card indices reveal that only a few pieces were weighed and photographs of selected few coins were put on index cards. Many coins being crudely struck, worn out and in an indifferent state of preservation, were not photographed and cards bear only their description. A serial number has been put on the back of the card indices which has been referred to by me in the description and reference of the coins in this work. The aforesaid article in the *Numismatic Digest* brought to light for the first time four coins depicting three-headed Śiva holding a club or trident-battleaxe in his right hand seated on a kneeling human figure, which was rightly identified as Apasmāra-purusha, with a female figure on his left and the Brāhmī legend *Bhagavata(/o) Chitreśvara Mahātmana(ḥ)* around on the obverse. The reverse depicted a deer to left or right bearing some subsidiary symbols above and below its back, facing *chaitya* or arched hill symbol or a female figure and having a railed tree behind. Though coins bearing single headed Śiva with the above-mentioned legend were known earlier, mostly from the British Museum collection, pieces showing tri-cephalous Śiva seated on Apasmāra-purusha presented an altogether new type. The said hoard contained numerous such coins. Unfortunately however, a complete study of this important hoard has remained a desideratum.

Covid-19 lockdown from March 2020 provided me an opportunity to devote time to study this hoard but the non-availability of photographs of all coins was a big impediment. Most of the coins being very crudely and partially struck and every piece appearing to be different from others was another reason to do justice to their study. So I took up the study of mono-cephalic and tri-cephalic Śiva-Chitreśvara type coins only for the present monograph. Since all photographs were not available, I have relied on the description of the coins on the card-indices in many cases. All credit therefore should go to the personnel who prepared the card indices. At places, however, I have used my own discretion to describe the varieties of coin-types. I have received immense help from the writings of earlier numismatists, Late Prof. Shastri in particular. This study would not have been possible without the help of Dr. K.K. Maheshwari, Mrs. Dr. Yogeshwari Shastri and Dr. Avinash Upadhyay to who all I express my gratitude. I have supplemented this study by including coins of Chitreśvara type from the collections of the British Museum and Shri Jan Lingen published by me earlier. Dr. Wilfried Pieper also included one such coin in his valuable book on *Ancient Indian Coins Revisited* published in 2013. Included in this work are coins from the collection of the Gurukula Museum, Jhajjar and those of the personal collection of Dr. K.K. Maheshwari (12 coins). The scans and details of the pieces in Maheshwari collection as well as 15 other coins in the INHCRF were kindly supplied by Dr. Amiteshwar Jha. I have also taken note of the coins put on the FB from time to time by some individuals, in the collections of Dr. Akshay Jain, Sarvashri Karan Singh, R.K. Aggarwal,

Amit Udeshi, Venki Iyer and Hardik Parekh as also pieces presented in some auctions. Dr. Suken Shah helped me in checking up some references and providing me scanned copies of some articles. I express my gratitude to all. Coins illustrated in this work are not to scale. The sizes and weights of the coins are, however, mentioned in known cases. Because of the crudeness of execution of most of the coins, their reproductions are not very clear in some cases but I could not help it and beg to be excused. I also apologize for the mistakes, omissions and commissions if any which may have crept in inspite of my best efforts.

Shri Vikas Arya and his expert and experienced team of the Aryan Books International owe my thanks for bringing out this monograph beautifully in its present form.

Devendra Handa
(devendrahanda@rediffmail.com)

Contents

Preface *vii*
Transliteration Table *xiii*

1. **Introduction** 1
Chitreśvara Type Coins 1

2. **Classification** 5
Class A: Uni-cephalic Chitreśvara Type 9
Type I: Uni-cephalic Chitreśvara/Deer to Left 9
Type II: Uni-cephalic Chitreśvara/Deer to Right 27
Class B: Tri-cephalous Chitreśvara Type 33
Type I: Tri-cephalous Chitreśvara/Deer to Left 34
Type II: Tri-cephalous Chitreśvara/Deer to Right 43
Class C: Indeterminate Deity Type 64
Type I 64

3. **The Devices and Iconographic Importance** 65

4. **Provenience, Date and Attribution** 70

Bibliography 85
Index 89

Transliteration Table

अ A, a	आ Ā, ā	इ I, i	ई Ī, ī	उ U, u
ऊ Ū, ū	ऋ Ṛi, ṛi	ऌ Ḷi, ḷi	ए E, e	ऐ Ai, ai
ओ O, o	औ Au, au	अं A/aṃ	अः Aḥ/aḥ	
क् K, k	ख् Kh, kh	ग् G, g	घ् Gh, gh	ङ् Ṅ, ṅ
च् Ch, ch	छ् Chh, chh	ज् J, j	झ् Jh, jh	ञ् Ñ, ñ
ट् Ṭ, ṭ	ठ् Ṭh, ṭh	ड् Ḍ, ḍ	ढ् Ḍh, ḍh	ण् Ṇ, ṇ
त् T, t	थ् Th, th	द् D, d	ध् Dh, dh	न् N, n
प् P, p	फ् Ph, ph	ब् B, b	भ् Bh, bh	म् M, m
य् Y, y	र् R, r	ल् L, l	व् V, v	श् Ś, ś
ष् Sh, sh	स् S, s	ह् H, h	क्ष् Ksh, ksh	त्र् Tr, tr
ज्ञ् Jñ, jñ	Jihvāmūlīya x	Upadhamānīya ≍	Avagraha ('), ऽ	

Common words and modern names are usually written without diacriticals.
In the original titles and quotations, Ṛ/ṛ, C/c and Ṣ/ṣ have also been used for ऋ, च् & ष्.

1

Introduction

CHITREŚVARA TYPE COINS

Chitreśvara type coins were first dug up along with many other coins (which were later attributed to the Kuṇindas, Yaudheyas, etc.) at Behat near Saharanpur in Uttar Pradesh while digging a canal in early 1834 by Captain P.T. Cautley (Superintendent, Doab Canal) and were forwarded to James Prinsep (1858: pp. 76-85, Pls. VII.4, XX.48) who published them drawing their figures in his own hands though their true importance was not known then nor were their legends deciphered properly.

Alexander Cunningham (1891: pp. 72-73) also discovered two copper coins of this type along with many other silver and copper coins from the area between Ambala and Saharanpur where such coins were found in greater number and illustrated them in Plate V.1-6 of his well known work on *Coins of Ancient India* listing all these coins under the tribal name Kuṇinda. The earliest of these coins (his Pl. V.6) bearing the Brāhmī legend *Kāḍasa* in Aśokan letters was regarded as 'of doubtful attribution' and two silver and a copper coin which contained the name of Kuṇinda (Pl. V.1-3) and the two later copper coins showing trident and battle-axe of Śiva without the tribal name (Pl. V.4-5) were attributed to the Kuṇinda tribe. The credit of reading the legends on these coins goes to Cunningham. The better one of the two copper coins bearing the figure of Śiva was described by him as following –

Æ, 0.8 inch, weight 181 grains, Author

Obv.: The God Śiva, standing to front with battle-axe trident in r. hand, and leopard skin hanging from l. arm. Indian legend, *Bhāgavato Chatreswara Mahātanā*.

Rev.: Deer in middle with symbol between horns, snake below to r., tree, star and vase to l. Chaitya and symbols.

The size of his second coin was 1 inch and it weighed 291 grains. The legend '*Bhāgavato Chatreśwara Mahātanā*' was later corrected to *Bhagavato Chitreśvara Mahātmanaḥ* meaning 'coin of the almighty Chitreśvara'. He also observed that these coins were extremely rare and he knew of only five specimens which all came 'from the west of Jumna' (Cunningham 1891: pp. 72-73, Pl. V.4-5).

Allan (1936: p. ciii) read the legend as 'Bhāgavata chatreśvara mahātmanaḥ' which has been accepted by most of the subsequent writers though with some minor variations. J.N. Banerjea (1956: p. 118) corrected Allan's reading of *Bhāgavata* as *bhagavata* and K.K. Dasgupta (1974: p. 99) as *bhagavataḥ*. No specimen, however, shows the use of the long medial vowel *ā* with the first letter. The last letter of this first word on many of the coins is clearly marked with the medial vowel *o* indicating that the first word of the legend was *bhagavato* and not *bhāgavata* or *bhagavataḥ* (Shastri, 1984: p. 30).

Some scholars took Chitreśvara to be the name of a Kuṇinda king (Altekar 1954: *Gupta-Vakataka Age*, p. 28; Chattopadhyaya 1958: p. 138). Allan did not explain the meaning and significance of the next word Chatreśvara. The word *chhatra* in Sanskrit means 'umbrella' which is the Indian insignia of sovereignty. Banerjea (1951: p. 163, fn. 2; 1956: p. 118; see also Banerjea 1957: pp. 797-98, fn. 7) accepted the legend with slight modification as Chatreśvara and proposed to restore it as

Chhatreśvara 'Lord of *Chhatra*' and took it to be an appellation of god Śiva and interpreted the legend as 'of the holy or worshipful one, the noble souled lord of the Chhatra'. He thought that "the tribal state of the Kuṇindas at one time was dedicated to the lord Śiva in the 2nd century AD and the coins were issued in his name in the capacity of a sovereign ruler." Earlier S.K. Chakrabortty (1931: p. 188) had also translated the legend as 'of Almighty Mahādeva, the lord, i.e. the coin dedicated to God Maheśvara' taking these coins as dedicatory in nature. Jai Prakash (1965: 127) pointed out that the legend does not contain any regal titles and all the words of the legend should be taken as the adjectives of Śiva whose figure appears on the coins bearing this legend. He opined that "In all probability, these coins were meant and issued to pass on as commemorative coins, to thank their god and to mark their independence. Most probably the Kuṇindas attributed their independence to Śiva, their tutelary deity." He translated the legend as 'óf the worshipful, noble-souled lord of the Chhatra (or Chhatreśvara).' Sircar (1968a: *The Age of Imperial Unity*, p. 161, fn. 1) opined that Chatra or Chhatra was the name of the Kuṇinda capital or its contraction for the purpose of writing.

Allan (1936: p. ciii) seems to have been influenced by the views of Cunningham and observed that Amoghabhūti "was probably an Indian chief who founded a short-lived kingdom at the close of the periods of Greek dominion in the Panjab in the last half of the first century BC which was soon swept away by the Śaka and Kushān invaders. The coinage of the Kuṇindas then disappears for nearly three centuries till the end of the second or in the third century AD we find coins again issued by a Kuṇinda republic. These are large pieces the module of which is suggested by the Kushān copper coins. The reverse revives the old Kuṇinda type of dear, tree, river, &c., and the obverse bears a figure of Śiva holding a trident and the legend: *Bhāgavata-chatreśvara-mahātmanaḥ*".

M.C. Joshi (1960: p. 49) pointed out that the absence of the sign indicating *i* or other vowels, is not uncommon in Indian numismatography and preferred to restore Chatreśvara as Chitreśvara and took it to be the name of Śiva as a *svayambhū-liṅga* (self-born or natural rock of the shape of phallic emblem) is still being worshipped under the name of Chitreśvara by the people of Gopeshwar near

Almora. It may be pointed out here that temples known as Chitreśvara Mahādeva Temple exists at Futa and Mall in Uttarakhand and another Shri Chitreshwar Shiv Mandir is located at village Chitreshwar on the bank of the river Suvarṇarekhā, obviously known after the old temple here, in Bahragora Block of district Singhbhum, Jharkhand. It houses the largest natural Śiva-liṅga in the 10th century temple built by Somavaṃśī or Keśarī dynasty of Odisha. Alleged to have been mentioned in the Utkala-khaṇḍa of the *Skandapurāṇa*, it is a famous temple for the popular belief that Lord Śiva fulfils the desires and wishes of all the devotees who visit it. A festival is celebrated here every year on the occasion of Śivarātri and Śiva-chaturdaśī (Wikipedia, s.v. Chitreshwar Temple). Dasgupta (1974: pp. 93-94) criticized Joshi's restoration and followed Banerjea pointing out that *Chhatra* is mentioned as the name of Śiva in the *Mahābhā*rata (Ray's ed. XIII.17, p. 1244 as referred to by Dasgupta) and that the name is current in other parts of India as well. He took Chatreśvara (for Chhatreśvara) to be due to a dialectical peculiarity of the region. It may, however, be pointed out here that at least two coins in the collection of the British Museum (Allan 1936: p. 118, nos. 73 and 76, Pl. XXIII.13 & 15) show the legend to be Chitreśvara which is also confirmed by a coin published by Prof Shastri. It may be pointed out here that there are quite a few specimens which clearly show the medial vowel *i* attached to the letter *ch* as we shall see subsequently and there should be absolutely no doubt now that the intended reading of the word was Chitreśvara and that it stood for the god Śiva depicted on the coins. Chitreśvara may be accepted as the phonetic peculiarity of the region and equated with god Chhatreśvara Śiva.

2

Classification

As referred to above, Prinsep got the earliest specimen of these coins from Behat and illustrated one coin in the form of a sketch (Prinsep 1858: Pl. VII.4) and Cunningham knew five pieces of which he described and illustrated two (1891: pp. 72-73, Pl. V.4-5). The British Museum collection of eleven Chitreśvara type coins comes from Nelson Wright, Spink, Rodgers, and Cunningham. On the basis of the arrangement and placement of the subsidiary symbols, Allan has distinguished three varieties of these anonymous coins (Allan 1936: pp. 167-68, Pls. XXIII.11-16; XLIII.14). A scrutiny of the coins in the British Museum enabled us to distinguish two more varieties (Handa 2001: pp. 25-26). Allan (1936: pp. 166-67, Pls. XXIII.11-16, XLIII.12-13) described eleven specimens divided into three varieties (Vars. a–c) illustrating 6 coins of Var. a showing deer to left, one coin each of Vars. b and c, the last one depicting the deer to right on the reverse. Dasgupta classified the British Museum coins listed by Allan under Class III of the Kuṇinda coins and divided them into eight varieties, A-H (Dasgupta 1974: pp. 93-94, CN 52-57, Pls. III.11-15, XLIII.12-13) without illustrating specimens of Vars. E and G. A new variety exists in the collection of Jan Lingen (Netherlands) (Handa 1994: pp. 25-26). L.C. Gupta obtained 27 coins from Tehri-Garhwal in January 1984 of which he published 15 pieces of Brahmaṇyadeva/Deer type. One of his coin was uni-cephalic Śiva-Chitreśvara type but L.C. Gupta attributed it as Kuṇinda specie (L.C. Gupta 1985: p. 17; 1986: p. 38, no. 6). All these coins surely belonged to the hoard which was discovered in early eighties of the last century referred to below in details.

Stray pieces exist here and there some of which have been put on the Facebook by some individuals. All these coins showed unicephalous Śiva standing holding the trident-axe in his right hand with the legend or part thereof along the margin on the obverse and a deer generally facing arched *chaitya* or hill/mountain, tree in railing behind (in one case above the deer) and undulating river line below with some subsidiary marks on the reverse.

As referred to in the Preface, a very important hoard consisting of Brahmaṇyadeva (Kārttikeya-Shashṭhī/Deer) and Śiva-Chitreśvara type coins was discovered in early eighties of the last century. It seems that it was disposed off in parts. The biggest part of more than two thousand coins was acquired by the Birla Archaeological and Cultural Research Institute, Hyderabad (BACRI). Some coins of this hoard reached even England and the British Museum acquired some pieces during 1983 and 1985 from Robert and Monica Tye. Early in 1981 Shri (now Dr.) K.K. Maheshwari got the BACRI hoard documented for INHCRF. Based on heresy, Prof. Shastri acknowledged Mandi district of western Himachal Pradesh to be its find spot. Dr. P.L. Gupta (1987: p. 31), however, observed that "The coins of both these types are not known earlier anywhere in this region. All the coins of both the types, known so far, are confined exclusively to the eastern part of Hariyana and the adjoining plains and the hilly regions of Uttar Pradesh" (now Uttarakhand). Dr. Gupta was, however, mistaken to regard 'the finds of Kuninda coins with Chitreśvara' from Sunet near Ludhiana, Karnal (Mitra 1875: p. 85), etc. Cunningham (*CASR*, XIV: p. 65, not 165 as mentioned by Gupta) has clearly mentioned '2 old Hindu coins of Amoghabhūti' from Sunet and Mitra (1875: 82-89) has described the coin from Karnal as belonging to Amoghabhūti type. Gupta wrongly identified three coins from Behat (Prinsep 1858: Pl. VII.1, 2 & 6) as of Chitreśvara type though Prinsep's Pl. VII.2 and Pl. XX.48 illustrated above surely belong to Chitreśvara type. In a small paper S.C. Kala (1946: pp. 36-37)) had brought to light the discovery of a hoard of 1000 Kuṇinda coins (not of about 10,000 coins as mentioned by Gupta 1987: p. 31) in the year 1880 in village Sumari, just above the town of Srinagar, the old capital of the Rajas of Garhwal and many more from Bhattisera and Devalgarh near Srinagar in the collection of Lala Manohar Lal of Srinagar. 164 Kārttikeya-Shashṭhī/Deer type coins (classified as Class 3 & 5 Yaudheya coins by Allan) were found earlier from Panjya in the Jaunsar-Bawar area of district Dehradun in 1936 (Dayal 1940: pp. 109-12) and a hoard of more than 119 coins was discovered from Lansdowne (Kala 1956, 46-48) in Garhwal region of Uttarakhand. L.C. Gupta (1985: pp. 14-17), as referred to above, also obtained from Tehri-Garhwal 27 coins which included Bramanyadeva (Kārttikeya-Shashṭhī/Deer) and Chitreśvara types. So the Garhwal area may have also been the probable provenance of this hoard and it is because of this reason that I have referred to it as the Garhwal Hoard (GH) which has been referred to earlier as the BACRI hoard in some writings.

As noted above this hoard also contained tri-cephalic Śiva-Chitreśvara type coins showing the god holding trident-battleaxe in his right hand with left akimbo seated on kneeling Apasmāra-purusha and attended by a female figure on the obverse and a stag or deer facing arched *chaitya* or a goddess with tree in railing on the other side on the reverse which was an unknown type till then. Prof. Shastri who published four of these coins with five others of interesting Kārttikeya-Shashṭhī/Deer type (Shastri 1984: pp. 24-34) stated that all the coins were die-struck copper coins and observed that "Except the Yaudheya coins with the god representation of a temple on the reverse, all the coins are of a thick and large fabric. They are circular or intended to be so. The devices and legends on most of these coins are very shallow: either the coin-blanks were not properly heated before striking or the engraving on the dies was shallow with the result that the dies had to be struck with great force. Consequently the coins have developed strong cracks, particularly along the edges" (*Ibid*: p. 24). P.L. Gupta too has observed that "All the coins are die-struck, but in all probability, both the obverse and reverse dies were not used simultaneously, which is the normal technique in producing die-struck coins. The appearance of the coins show that only one die was perhaps used at a time, i.e. the planchets were placed on the anvil having no die; and the obverse die was placed on the planchet and hammered. Thus the obverse was stamped first; later the planchet, so stamped, was turned to the other side so the stamped side was on the anvil and over the planchet was placed the reverse die and hammered again. Consequently, the motifs particularly of the obverse, have lost their sharpness and the planchets have become a little concave. Besides the absence of sharpness, the entire motif, in its perfect form is not available on any side. It also appears that tongs were perhaps used to hold the planchets during the hammering process. The tongs thus seem to have left their impressions on some of the coins; hereby they indicate that the metal of the planchet was most likely malleable. This crude method, used for the coins, suggests that the mint-people were not well conversant with the double die striking technique" (Gupta 1987: p. 33). Following Cunningham and Allan, Prof. Shastri attributed all coins of this hoard representing standing Śiva and the newly found type of tri-cephalous god seated on a supine human figure with the legend *Bhagavata Ch(i)treśvara Mahātmanaḥ* or part of it to the Kuṇindas assigning them to the post-Amoghabhūti period after a gap of more than two centuries after Amoghabhūti's silver specie. Prof. Shastri observed further that "Both the Kuninda and Yaudheya coins present a large number of hitherto unnoticed varieties and help in solving some of the baffling problems facing numismatists interested in these coinages" (*Ibid.*).

The Covid-19 lockdowns from March 25, 2020 onwards prompted me to study the card indices again and because of my limitations of growing age I have taken up only the study of Chitreśvara type coins though a good majority of the coins of this hoard belong to the Kārttikeya-Shashṭhī and Kārttikeya-Deer types of the Yaudheyas with many new features and varieties and may form the subject of another monograph. Though the hoard may have contained numerous varieties of the tri-cephalous Śiva-Chitreśvara type coins, I have been able only to distinguish quite a few newer varieties from the card indices and few photographs on them, all credit for which should go to Prof. Shastri and his son Dr. Avinash Upadhyay.

Taking stock of all published coins including ten pieces which I had examined in the reserve collection of the British Museum and brought to light earlier, I had attributed the Chitreśvara type coins to the Yaudheyas (Handa 1996: pp. 81-85, Pls. I.3-8 and II.1-3; 1999: 33-43; 2007: pp. 245-56, Pls. LXXVIII-LXXXIV). Some scholars, individuals and Auction Houses, however, still continue to refer to them as Kuṇinda coins. I have studied all published and unpublished Chitreśvara type coins to classify them afresh and attributed them to the Yaudheya with additional evidence.

CLASS A: UNI-CEPHALIC CHITREŚVARA TYPE

Type I: Uni-cephalic Chitreśvara/Deer to Left

Var. 1

Obv.: A male figure (Śiva) standing facing, holding trident with axe on shaft in right hand, left hand akimbo, leopard skin hanging from left arm, flower or star behind over his left shoulder with Brāhmī legend *Bhagavata Chitreśvara-Mahātmaṇ*a(*ḥ*) (restored on the cumulative evidence) [- -] with the legend beginning from about 2 o'clock to 10 o' clock position with a gap between 5 and 7 o' clock betraying its disposition as ( ).

Rev.: Deer to left with *śrīvatsa* ( ) above horns, tree-in-railing ( ) behind, six-arched *chaitya* capped by an umbrella and an inverted loop and having a triangle-headed staff (*Indradhvaja*) below in front ( ), a square ( ) below the deer, a vase over another symbol ( ) above, traces of a *svastika* on the right of the preceding symbol and a wavy line ( ) below, all within a border of dots.

Ref.: British Museum (BM): p. 167, no. 70, Pl. XXII.12 (2.5 cm, 17.972 g).

What has been drawn as (*tra*) by Allan is actually (*tma*) as seen on many coins.

Var. 2

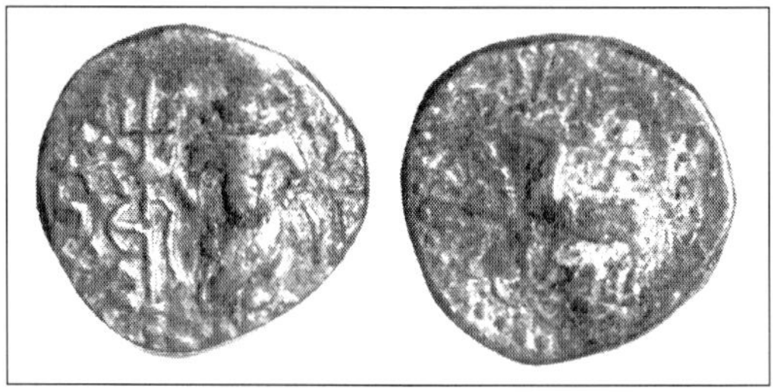

Obv.: Similar but the trident-axe has a long tassel, the letter *ch* here has the medial vowel mark *i* indicating the word to be *chitreśvara*.

Rev.: Same as above but the deer has an elongated *śrīvatsa* with a vertical line between the *nāga*-like symbols  between the horns. The symbol below the triangular six-arched *chaitya* looks like *Indradhvaja* but is not very clear, all within a border of dots.

Ref.: BM: p. 167, no. 73 (2.5 cm, 18.83 g).

Var. 3

Obv.: Same as on Var. 1 above but Śiva has a *chhatra* or canopy-like turban () on the head and six-petalled lotus on his left shoulder, animal skin hanging from the left art with only traces of the inscription.

Rev.: Deer to left with  below, six-arched *chaitya* having a four-compartmented pedestal and surmounted by a *nandipada* at the back, vase (), railed tree with three horizontal branches () and a vertically placed wavy line (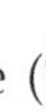) above the back and *śrīvatsa* between the horns.

Ref.: BM: p. 168, no. 78, Pl. XXIII.11 (2.456 cm, 17.754 g). See also Smith 1906, 170, no. 36.

Following Allan, Dasgupta too has wrongly drawn the figure of the *chaitya* as , but it has got only one tiered pedestal comprising four square compartments.

The legend seems to have started at about 2 to about 10 o'clock position with a gap between 5 and 7 under the feet of the god.

Var. 4

Obv.: As above but the shaft of the trident-battleaxe slanting to left towards the top and the legend starting with *Bhagavata* from about 2 o'clock position clearly visible indicating its continuation up to 10 o'clock position with a gap between 5 and 7 o'clock (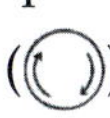).

Rev.: As above, *śrīvatsa* () between horns of the deer; the lower end of the tail of the deer forms a lozenge, railed tree and vertical undulating line () above the vase are notable features as on the preceding example, dotted border around.

Ref.: Dr. Akshay Jain collection (17.220 g, 24 mm).

Var. 5

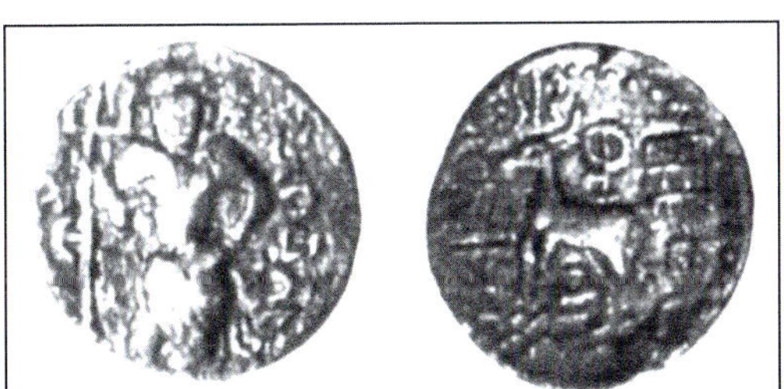

Obv.: Same as on Var. 3 above but the lotus on left shoulder represented by dots.

Rev.: As on Var. 1, but the *chaitya* before the deer is surmounted by a *nandipada*, the *śrīvatsa* between the horns of the deer (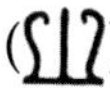) is elongated, the vase is shown below the deer,  symbol on the back changes to a mirror form like . Tree in railing lies at the back of the deer and there is a border of dots.

Ref.: BM: p. 167, no. 70a, Pl. XLIII.13 (2.5 cm, 17.171 g).

Var. 6

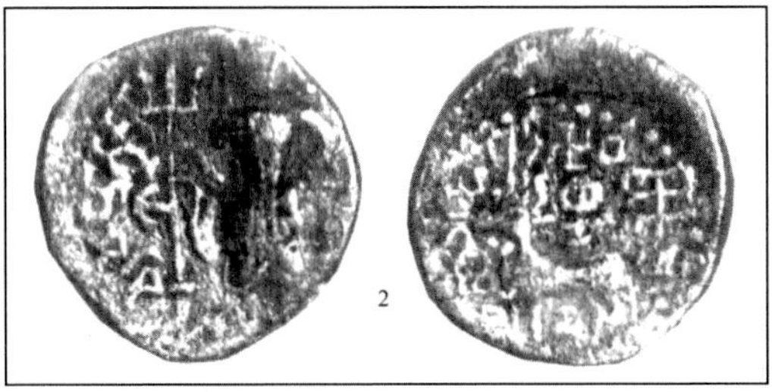

Obv.: Same as above but the fragmentary legend '. . . *vara-mahātmana(ḥ*)*' between 7 and 11 o'clock is quite clear, the vertically placed trident-axe in Śiva's right hand has a long tassel.

Rev.: Same as above but the symbol  has a *svastika* above and □ to the right of that, there seems to be a vase under the deer; the whole reverse device has been struck with force giving the impression of an incuse, beaded border around.

Ref.: BM: p. 167, no. 71 (2.5 cm, 18.144 g).

Var. 7

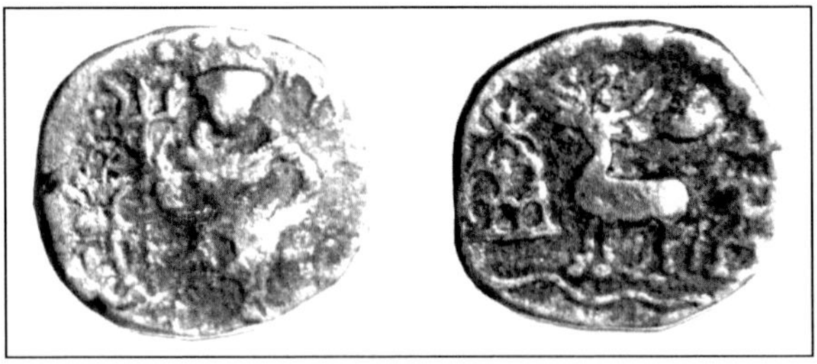

Obv.: Same as above within a border of dots.
Rev.: Deer to left facing a six-arched *chaitya*, probably garlanded, surmounted by a trident or *nandipada* but without triangle-headed standard below, *śrīvatsa* between the horns and vase at the back of the animal, tree in railing behind, wavy line below, all within dotted border.
Ref.: BM: p. 168, no. 74, Pl. XLIII.12 (2.364 cm, 16.107 g).

Var. 8

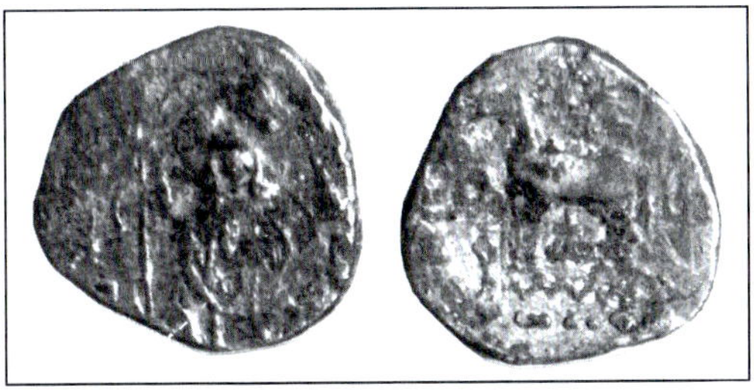

Obv.: Same as above.
Rev.: Same as above but the subsidiary symbols are badly worn out except inverted *Indradhvaja* below the deer.
Ref.: BM: p. 168, no. 75 (2.6 cm, 18.216 g).

Allan and following him Dasgupta also, has wrongly drawn the symbol below the deer.

Var. 9

Obv.: As above with the legend almost completely preserved from 1 to 11 o'clock position with the last letter *na* between the spikes of the trident and the head of the god, medial vowel mark *i* clearly attached to *ch* making it *chi*, the dotted lotus or star mark on the left shoulder of the god is missing here and the right hand of the god is bent at elbow and raised to the level of the shoulder in *abhaya* (fear-allaying posture) rather than holding the shaft of the trident-battleaxe which stands independently on left.

Rev.: Six-arched hill with a parasol is surmounted by *nandipada* symbol and has the triangle-headed symbol below, the deer has the square box below and four-branched tree in railing behind; the horns of the stag are widespread and has looped type of *śrīvatsa* (88) between them; vase is shown above the tree and eight-pronged star is depicted between the vase and the *śrīvatsa*. Border of dots is visible on a large portion of the flan and the round die impression is incused.

Ref.: BM: p. 168, no. 76, Pl. XXIII.15 (2.274 cm, 8.449 g).

Var. 10

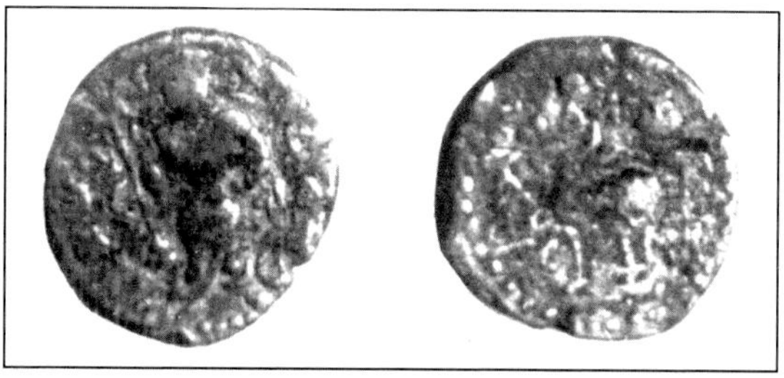

Obv.: Same as above but the god seems to be a bit corpulent.

Rev.: Same as above but the vase above the tree is different.

Ref.: BM: p. 168, no. 77, Pl. XXIII.15 (2.15 cm, 8.495 g).

Var. 11

Obv.: Same as above with Śiva holding filleted trident-axe and almost perfect legend *Bhagavata Chitreśvara Mahātmana(ḥ)*. The legend is disposed from 1 to 11 o' clock with a gap between 5 and 7 o' clock position (◯).

Rev.: As above but the *nandipada* above the *chaitya* seems to have been counter marked by the star mark and the symbol under the deer looks like Brāhmī *yya*-like variety of the *śrīvatsa*.

Ref.: BM: p. 167, no. 72, Pl. XXIII.14 (2.672 cm, 17.104 g).

Var. 12

Obv.: As Var. 3 above showing curled locks of hair falling on the shoulders of Śiva.

Rev.: As above but parasoled six-arched hill has three dots above it in two tiers of two and one, the head of the deer has a *svastika* above; the vase on the back of the deer has bold *śrīvatsa* symbol above it; triangle-headed symbol below the hill symbol and square box (□) below the deer are clearly struck and the river line below has many undulations. The stem of the three branched tree rises from the base of the square shaped railing on right. Border of dots has survived on a good portion of the reverse.

Ref.: Lingen collection (2.5 cm, 18.35 g).

Var. 13

Obv.: As above with almost complete and clear figure of Śiva holding trident-battleaxe in his right hand with shaft at slightly acute angle and left akimbo supporting animal skin on the forearm, wearing dhoti with clearly marked folds, turban indicated by pellets and locks falling down, dotted star on left shoulder, legend starting at about 2.30 o'clock and ending at 10 o'clock position with a gap between 5 and 7 o'clock as .

Rev.: As above but *śrīvatsa* having an elongated vertical between curved *nāga*-like strokes between the horns of the deer who has an elongated horizontal prognathism, on the back of the deer has a crescent with star above it.

Ref.: Hardik Parekh collection, 17.40 g.

Var. 14

Obv.: As above but the god is depicted as wearing a torque and sacred thread of Rudrāksha beads, multiple bangles, *karṇa-kuṇḍalas* 'earrings', dhoti secured by *netrasūtra* 'waist band', has a six-petalled lotus symbol on the left shoulder and holds the trident-battleaxe with its top bent towards his face. The legend runs from 2 to 10 o'clock as usual with a gap between 5 and 7 o'clock position.

Rev.: As above but there is a vase above and *svastika* on right above the tree in railing.

Ref.: Karan Singh collection.

This coin-type seems to have been the commonest and specimens illustrated by Mitchiner (1976, p. 633, Type 931, 18.02 g; Zeno 218162) may well be compared with it.

Var. 15

Obv.: As above, trident-battleaxe with long tassel on the right held vertically, seven dot star on left shoulder, circular earring in left ear, slightly splayed feet of the god and legend beginning at 2 o'clock position with *bhagavata chitre* between 2 and 5 and *śvara mahātmana* between 7 and 10 o'clock position.

Rev.: As above but the six-arched symbol has an inverted triangle-headed symbol above it and normal triangle-headed symbol below it, *śrīvatsa* without vertical line () between the horns,  symbol on the back of the deer having a vase and *svastika* above, square box under the deer, the tree in railing at the back of the deer with looped tail has three horizontal branches with leaves falling downwards, traces of undulating line below and dotted border around.

Ref.: R.K. Aggarwal collection, 18.2 g.

Var. 16

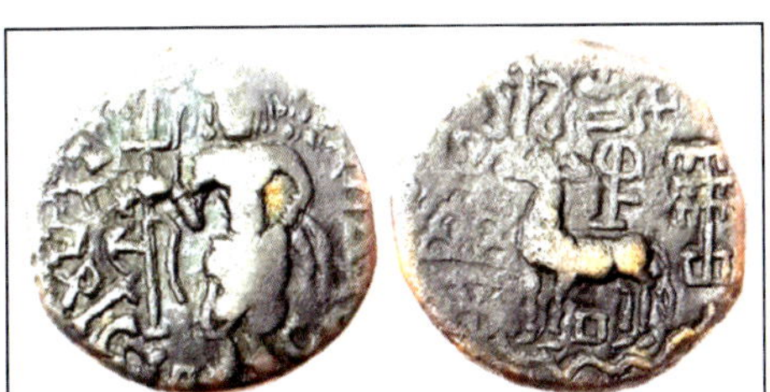

Obv.: As above but different strands of locks falling from the turban on shoulders.

Rev.: As above but *Indradhvaja* above and below the multi-arched *chaitya*, *śrīvatsa* with vertical line between horns, vase having rectangular base.

Ref.: R.K. Aggarwal collection, 18.1 g.

This coin seems almost similar to the former but the face of the god, the base of the vase and the animal skin betray die difference.

Var. 17

Obv.: The god standing to front as usual on a serrated pedestal holding the weapon in right hand with left akimbo.

Rev.: Deer to left with railed tree behind surmounted by a *svastika*,  above the deer and square box below.

Ref.: Garhwal Hoard: Negative no. 380/1-2, card no. 146.

Var. 18

Obv.: The well preserved coin shows almost complete die impression showing the enface standing god with feet splayed outwards, wearing dhoti secured by waist-band, upper garment, necklace, wristlets and turban; traces of beaded sacred thread are also visible. He is holding with his right hand the shaft of the trident with battleaxe attached to it on the left and the left hand of the god is resting on hip with lion-skin hanging from the arm. There is a seven-pronged star on his left shoulder. The tree in railing on right has four horizontal branches with drooping leaves. The legend from 1.30 to 10 o'clock with a gap between 5 and 7 o'clock ( ) is clear except that the upper parts of the letters are slightly out of flan on the left showing clearly the *i-mātrā* attached to *ch*.

Rev.: As above but without *nandipada* over parasoled *chaitya*, triangle-headed symbol below *chaitya*, horns of the deer wide spread with looped *śrīvatsa* ( ) between them, no symbol between the legs of the deer but undulating line below, four-branched broad tree in railing behind the deer and vase above the back of the deer, all within dotted border.

Ref.: Karan Singh collection, 17.22 g. See also Pieper 2015: p. 51, Fig. 16.

Var. 19

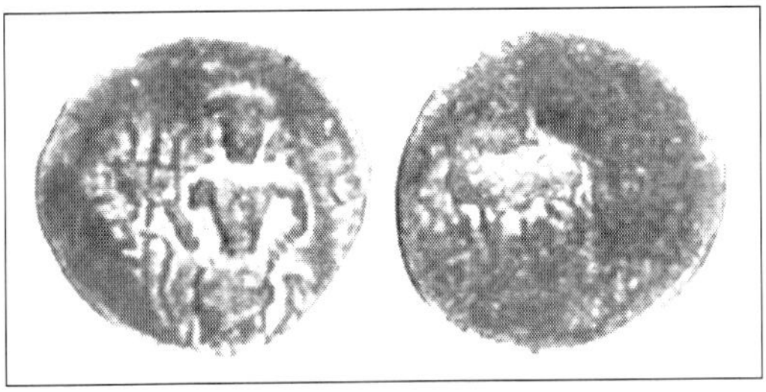

Obv.: Turbaned Śiva standing facing holding in his right hand tasseled battle-axe slightly turned inwards towards its top with left hand wearing multiple bangles and supporting leopard skin hanging from the forearm, lotus on left shoulder and partially visible legend around beginning from about 2 o'clock position.

Rev.: Deer to left facing six-arched hill having lotus below, vase and *śrīvatsa* above the back of deer, tree symbol with four horizontal branches behind and *Indradhvaja* below the deer.

Ref.: Marudhar Arts, Auction 32, October 2020, Lot no. 14, 17.50 g, 25.20 mm.

Var. 20

Obv.: Śiva standing to front with feet splayed at right angles, holding trident-battleaxe in right hand, left hand on hip, almost complete legend in big Brāhmī letters *(Bhaga)vata chitreśva(ra) mahātma(naḥ)* from 11 to 10 o'clock position with a gap between 5 to 7 o'clock position .

Rev.: Deer to left facing multi-arched hill with river line flowing towards the right, railed tree behind the deer, *svastika* on its back and inverted *Indradhvaja* below, border of dots.

Ref.: National Museum collection (Ray 2010: p. 229, Fig. 11.13).

Var. 21

Obv.: God standing facing holding trident-axe in right hand and left resting on hip with animal-skin hanging from the forearm as usual, feet of the god splayed at right angles, traces of legend on right but *mahā* visible at 9-10, beaded border.

Rev.: Deer with long legs facing multi-arched *chaitya*, *svastika* above the deer and an unusual symbol () below the deer, border of dots.

Ref.: Garhwal Hoard: Negative no. 380/2-7-8; card no. 175; 8.905 g, 21 mm.

Another coin of this variety in the Garhwal Hoard (Negative no. 382/3-1, card no. 312, 9.985 g, 22 mm) preserves the Brāhmī legend – *Chitreśva* – from 2 to 4 o'clock position in bold letters clearly on the obverse and *svastika* on the back of the deer on the reverse –

Var. 22

Obv.: Similar with trident-axe closer to the body and legend *Bhagavato* starting from 11 o'clock () struck with a different die.

Rev.: Traces of device with deer to left and railed tree on right, symbols above and below the deer not clearly visible, all within dotted border.

Ref.: Garhwal Hoard: Negative no. 382/3-3, card no. 314, 8.870 g, 23 mm.

Var. 23

Obv.: God standing as above but with the shaft of the trident-axe inclined away from the face and the clearly visible legend *Ch(i)tresvara mahā* from about 1 to 5 o'clock indicating its disposition as above ( ).

Rev.: Deer to left facing crudely drawn arched symbol with parasol above and *Indradhvaja* below, *svastika* placed above the railed tree (visible only in traces) and not on the back of the deer, no symbol visible under the deer.

Ref.: Dr. Akshay Jain collection (10.570 g, 21 mm).

Var. 24

Obv.: God wearing beaded *yajñopavīta* 'sacred thread' standing facing as if cross-legged with both feet turned towards right, bracelet on left wrist, the legend starts at about 1 o'clock position and the shaft of the trident-battleaxe is inclined inwards towards the top.

Rev.: Deer to left facing three-arched *chaitya* surmounted by a parasol, *śrīvatsa* ( ) between the horns of the deer and vase above its back, traces of railed tree on right, all within border of dots.

Ref.: Amit Udeshi collection, 18.28 g.

Var. 25

Obv.: Śiva standing cross-legged to front as above with traces of star or lotus mark on left shoulder and legend *–gavatach-* - from 2 to 4 o'clock.

Rev.: As above but the form of the *chaitya* and railed tree differ and there is an undulating river line below.

Ref.: Handa 2007: Pl. LXXXI.2.

Var. 26

Obv.: Śiva standing enface with lotus mark on left shoulder, the device seems to have been struck over an earlier piece and shows the retrograde legend *'mahātmana'* from 4 to 1 o'clock position betraying the disposition of the legend as .

Rev.: Same as above but there is a dotted lotus symbol under the *chaitya*, vase with and *śrīvatsa* on right above on the back of the deer and inverted *Indradhvaja* below the deer.

Ref.: Gurukula Museum, Jhajjar collection.

Var. 27

Obv.: As above but the complete legend is retrograde from 10 to 2 o'clock position with gap from 7 to 5 o'clock confirming the disposition of the retrograde legend as above ().

Rev.: Six-arched *chaitya* surmounted by *nandipada* with dotted star or lotus below, inverted *Indradhvaja* between the legs of the deer, vase with above and railed tree capped by bold *śrīvatsa* symbol at the back of the deer, long tail of the deer ending in lozenge shape, devices struck very neatly.

Ref.: Trade/Internet. CA Mitresh Singh had put this coin on the Facebook from the collection of Shri Vivek Singh.

Var. 28

Obv.: God standing as usual, retrograde legend *vatochitreśva* on right with clearly marked medial vowel mark on *ch*.

Rev.: Deer to left facing *chaitya*, inverted *Indradhvaja* below the deer and square vase and another star-like symbol above.

Ref.: Garhwal Hoard: Negative no. 382/2-20, 2.2 cm, 11.895 g, card no. 307.

Var. 29

Obv. As usual but partly obliterated, *Chitreś(v)a*- - - on left from bottom upwards from about 8 o' clock position in letters of larger size indicating that the legend may have continued to about 4 or 5 o'clock position (), border of dots.

Rev.: Deer to left facing a multi-arched *chaitya* with parasol above and *svastika* on its back.

Ref.: Garhwal Hoard: Negative no. 382/2-24, 2.2 cm, 9.835 g, card no. 311.

Var. 30

Obv.: Śiva bearing three roundish pods of locks on head standing enface with right hand held in *abhaya-mudrā* 'fear-allaying posture' and left on hip supporting the animal-skin, trident-battleaxe on left; letter *bha* at 7 o'clock position indicating the disposition of the legend as above (◯), beaded border.

Rev.: Only hind part of the deer to left visible with dotted lotus above its back and inverted tree on right (at the back of the deer), all within dotted border.

Ref.: Garhwal Hoard: Negative no. 380/1-8, card no. 149.

Var. 31

Obv.: As above, legend *Mahātmana(ḥ)* on left from bottom upwards.

Rev.: Deer to left facing *chaitya* with flowing channel, railed tree at the back, big *svastika* above the deer and ⊥ below.

Ref.: Garhwal Hoard: Negative no. 380/2-10, 2.2 cm, 9.565 g, card no. 177.

Var. 32

Obv.: Partly visible device of the god standing with left hand on hip, part of the legend - - -*vatachatreś*- -.

Rev.: Deer standing to left facing 6-arched hill from the base of which flows a channel, traces of tree in railing on right and a symbol above the back of the deer and  below.

Ref.: Garhwal Hoard: card no. 1/42; no. 518 also shows river emanating from the hill symbol.

Var. 33

Obv.: Śiva with parasol-like head gear (), standing as usual holding the trident which has inverted spikes as well ().

Rev.: Deer facing to left the *chaitya* with *svastika* above the head and square box at the back.

Ref.: Garhwal Hoard: card no. 1/47; 1/49 shows *chitreśva* also on the obverse.

Var. 34

Obv.: God standing as usual, legend - - - *chatreśvara*- - -.

Rev.: Deer to left with *triratna* above its back.

Ref.: Garhwal Hoard: card no. 1/52; no. 379 shows traces of railed tree on right and also river line below.

Var. 35

Obv.: God standing facing holding trident-axe in right hand with left akimbo, Brāhmī letters *śvara* visible on right and *ma* on left.

Rev.: Deer to left facing *chaitya*, railed tree on right, river line below, inverted *triratna* above the back of the deer and Brāhmī *ku*-like symbol () below the deer.

Ref.: Garhwal Hoard: card nos. 506, 513.

Var. 36

Obv.: God standing as usual, traces of the legend.

Rev.: Deer facing *chaitya* on left with vase with foliage () above the back of the deer.

Ref.: Garhwal Hoard: card nos. 520-521; no. 763 shows *chitreśva* on right edge of the obverse and also a beaded border around.

Var. 37

Obv.: God as usual, legend from top left to right *Bhagavata cha_-_.*

Rev.: Deer to left facing hill symbol, railed tree on right, symbol below the deer and *svastika* above the back.

Ref.: Garhwal Hoard: card no. 502; no. 507 shows beaded border also and 508 shows traces of river line too below.

TYPE II: UNI-CEPHALIC CHITREŚVARA/DEER TO RIGHT

Var. 1

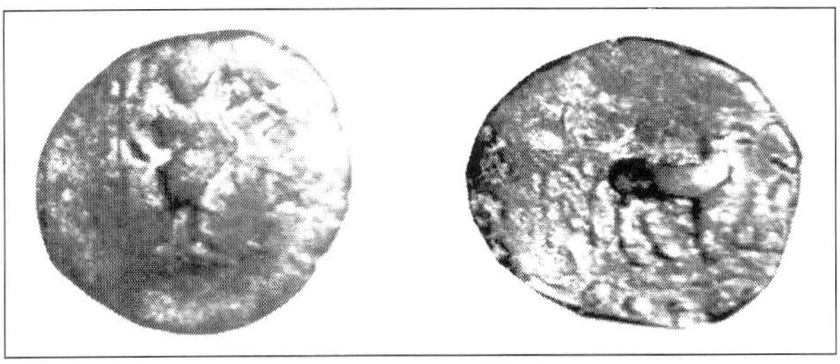

Obv.: Enface god standing holding trident-battleaxe in his right hand with left on hip traces of inscription on right.

Rev.: Deer to right, on left and on right. Other symbols above and below the deer are not clear.

Ref.: BM: p. 168, no. 79, Pl. XLIII.14, Rev. only (2.491 cm, 17.77 g).

The coin is in a very indifferent state of preservation. It seems that the reverse has been struck on an earlier coin as a very light impression of a deer can be seen at the back of the present figure.

Var. 2

Obv.: Traces of the god standing as usual but without the weapon, legend *vatachitre* from 8.30 to 11 o'clock indicating its beginning at 7 o'clock position (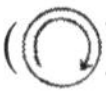).

Rev.: Deer with long legs and vertically elongated neck to right facing three-tiered arched symbol with parasol above having river line emanating from its base.

Ref.: Garhwal Hoard: Negative no. 382/3-4, card no. 315, 7.105 g, 22 mm.

Var. 3

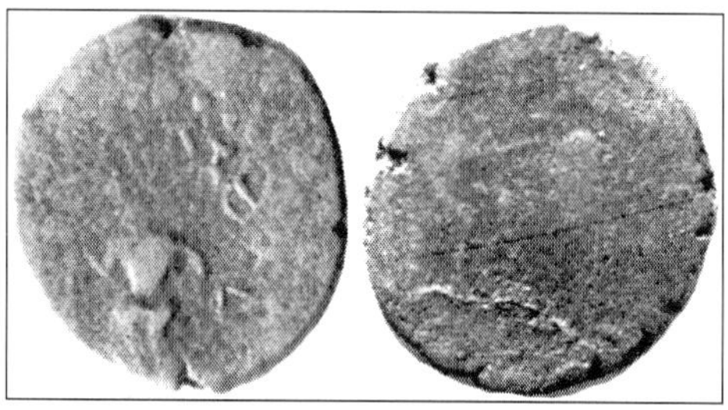

Obv.: God standing as usual, part of the legend – vatochi- visible at 1–3 o'clock position indicating its beginning at about 10–11 o'clock (),border of dots visible in the top portion.

Rev.: Traces of deer to right with undulating line below.

Ref.: Garhwal Hoard: Negative no. 382/3-7, card no. 318, 8.115 g, 20 x 22 mm.

Var. 4

Obv.: The main device within the beaded border is defaced with traces of a female with left hand raised and right akimbo may have stood to the left of the tricephalous god, Brahmi letters hat(ma) at 2–3 o'clock indicates that the legend started at about 10–11 o'clock and may have been disposed as ◯.

Rev.: Deer with long legs standing to right facing female deity, the head of the deer and the bust of the female figure are truncated, part of the beaded border visible.

Ref.: Garhwal Hoard: Negative no. 380/8-10, card no. 321, 10.960 g, 22 mm.

Another coin though badly mutilated (INHCRF-14, 8.11 g, 23 x 23 mm) shows a similar legend pattern with *gavatachitresvara* visible from 12 to 5 o'clock position –

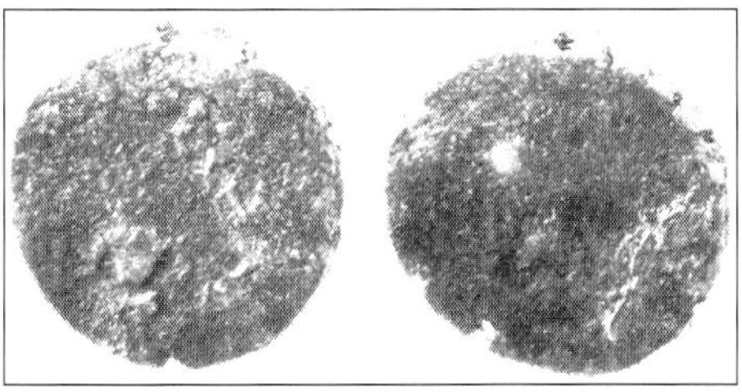

Var. 5

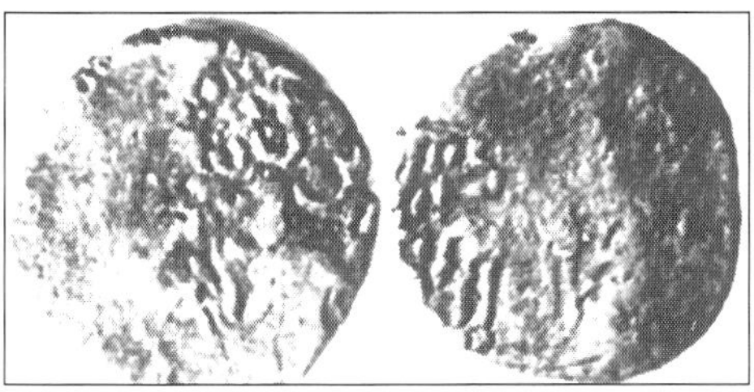

Obv.: As above, part of the legend - - - *tachitre*- - - from 1 to 2 o'clock position.

Rev.: As above but a channel flowing from the base of the hill symbol, *svastika* above the deer, partly visible tree on left.

Ref.: Garhwal Hoard: Negative no. 382/2-22, 2.3 cm, 10.305 g, card no. 309.

Var. 6

Obv.: As above.

Rev.: Deer to right facing hill symbol, ⌶ tree in railing on left, symbol below the deer.

Ref.: Garhwal Hoard: card no. 1/55.

Var. 7

Obv.: As above.
Rev.: As above but *svastika* and inverted *triratna* above the back of the deer.
Ref.: Garhwal Hoard: card no. 745.

Var. 8

Obv.: As above.
Rev.: As above but  symbol between the legs of deer.
Ref.: Garhwal Hoard: card no. 1/40.

Var. 9

Obv.: As above.
Rev.: As above but *śrivatsa* above the deer.
Ref.: Garhwal Hoard: card no. 1/38; 361 and 505 also show *svastika* above the deer.

Var. 10

Obv.: As above but the shaft of the trident has inverted semi-circular appendage () below the spikes.
Rev.: As no. 1 above.
Ref.: Garhwal Hoard: card no. 1/36.

Var. 11

Obv.: As above but the trident in the right hand of the god is .
Rev.: Deer to right facing a human figure (goddess) standing with left hand on hip and right hand raised to the level of the shoulder (probably holding lotus by its stalk).
Ref.: Garhwal Hoard: 9.510 g, 20 mm, card no. 1/2.

Var. 12

Obv.: God as above but female figure may also be made out on the right.
Rev.: Deer standing to right with *triratna* above its head and a vase on back, rest effaced.
Ref.: Garhwal Hoard: 9.840 g, 20 mm, card no. 1/8.

Var. 13

Obv.: As no. 1 above but reversed legend *Bhagavatacha*- - -.
Rev.: As above, river line below, inverted *triratna* above the head of the deer, traces of lined border.
Ref.: Garhwal Hoard: card no. 376; no. 745 has similar reverse but the legend on the obverse is not clear.

Var. 14

Obv.: Large part is obliterated but the legend *bhagavata cha* can be made out clearly.
Rev.: Hind part of the deer standing to right with *śrīvatsa* above.
Ref.: Garhwal Hoard: card no. 1/38.

Var. 15

Obv.: Similar with the letters *chitra* on the obverse.
Rev.: Similar but dumb-bell below the deer.
Ref.: Garhwal Hoard: card no. 1/50.

Var. 16

Obv.: As above, partially visible legend - - *vatacha* - - -.
Rev.: Deer to right facing arched symbol of a different type (), *svastika* above the back of the deer.
Ref.: Garhwal Hoard: card nos. 354, 356.

Var. 17

Obv.: As usual with part of the legend *chataśva* visible.
Rev.: Deer to right facing a hill symbol from which originates a river channel.
Ref.: Garhwal Hoard: card no. 387. Card no. 340 shows a triangular hill with river line.

Var. 18

Obv.: Śiva standing slightly turned to his right holding trident-battleaxe in his right hand with left on waist, legend on right – [*ch(i)tra(/e)śva*]*ramahat-* - - from about 1 to 4–5 o'clock. The first part of the legend (i.e. *Bhagavata*) is worn out but seems to have been placed on the left between 10 and 1 o'clock position indicating the disposition of the legend from about 10 to 5 o'clock position ().

Rev.: Deer to right facing three-arched *chaitya* (probably with a parasol above), inverted tree with downcast branches at the back of the deer with vertically hanging long tail and river line below.

Ref.: Garhwal Hoard: Negative No. 381/1-2, card no. 217, 10.170 g, 24 mm.

Var. 19

Obv.: Worn out figure of the god standing facing with left hand akimbo and *chitreśvara* (*maha*) visible between 12.30 and 5 o' clock position. The legend thus seems to have begun at about 10 o'clock and continued to about 9 o'clock position with a gap between 5 and 7 o'clock ().

Rev.: As above.

Ref.: Garhwal Hoard: Negative No. 381/1-8, card no. 223, 10.065 g, 23 mm.

Var. 20

Obv.: Śiva wearing *ardhoruk* 'undergarment covering the thighs' standing slightly turned to his right holding trident-battleaxe in his right hand with left on waist, retrograde legend *Bhaga*- - - - starting at 4 o'clock ().

Rev.: Deer to right having comparatively shorter tail with slantingly placed inverted tree on the back, undulating line below.

Ref.: Venki Iyer's collection (obtained from Marudhar Arts, e-Auction 30, Lot no. 15, 11.20 g. Venki has informed me that it is 25 x 21 mm in size and 3.3 mm in thickness.

We thus see that coins showing the deer to right are comparatively rarer. These coins seem to have been struck carelessly initially but later attention was paid for better striking. They have been issued in two denominations of 160 and 80 *rattīs* (18.5 and 9.25 g approximately). The flans of some coins were probably properly heated before being struck and the cracks on the edges are few. Though only a limited number of good specimens of this type are available they show that the dies were changed very frequently. The die-cutters were not very experienced as indicated by their crudeness and retrograde legends but with the passage of time they got experienced to accommodate properly a large number of devices and symbols as also to provide relief to the figures. The legend generally begins at about 2 o'clock position and ends at about 10 o'clock position with a gap from 5 to 7 o' clock under the feet of the god but variations are there as indicated by some coins.

CLASS B: TRI-CEPHALOUS CHITREŚVARA TYPE

As noted above, Prof. Ajay Mitra Shastri published in 1984 four coins of the new type showing tri-cephalous Śiva seated on Apasmāra-purusha from this Garhwal Hoard. These are round or irregularly round copper coins having the following sizes and weights: (1) 2.0 x 2.2 cm, 8.625 g; (2) 2.2 cm, 9.6 g; (3) 2.1 cm, 8.54 g and (4) 2.3 x 2.5 cm, 10.195g, all half units. Ten pieces of this type were acquired by the British Museum in the eighties of the last century. They are similar to the coins of the Garhwal Hoard and may have originally belonged to the same hoard. Depending upon the direction to which the deer on the reverse faces, these coins may be divided into two types and may be described as following on the cumulative evidence of the specimens which are generally struck very carelessly like the hex-cephalic Kārttikeya type coins and are in an extremely indifferent state of preservation.

Being carelessly struck and in an indifferent condition we hardly come across any specimen which gives us a complete impression of the dies. Generally the devices are either only partially accommodated or have not come out at all due to defective striking. No coin shows the complete legend and it is only on the cumulative evidence that we give below what these coins may have actually been.

Obv.: Three-headed Śiva holding a club or a trident in his right hand with left placed on the respective knee, seated on Apasmāra-purusha, with a female figure on right holding a flower (or a twig of flowers) in her raised right hand and left resting on the hip, having (often very fragmentary) Brāhmī legend around *Bhagavata(ḥ) Chitreśvara-Mahātmaṇa(ḥ)*.

Rev.: Deer to right or left, generally having a *śrīvatsa* between the horns, triangle-headed standard below and *svastika* and/or some other symbol above the back, facing a female figure in front.

Type I: Tri-cephalous Chitreśvara/Deer to Left

On the basis of the direction of the deer on the reverse the coins are distinguished as of two types. Of the four coins published by Prof. Shastri only one depicted the deer to left. He described it as follows.

Var. 1

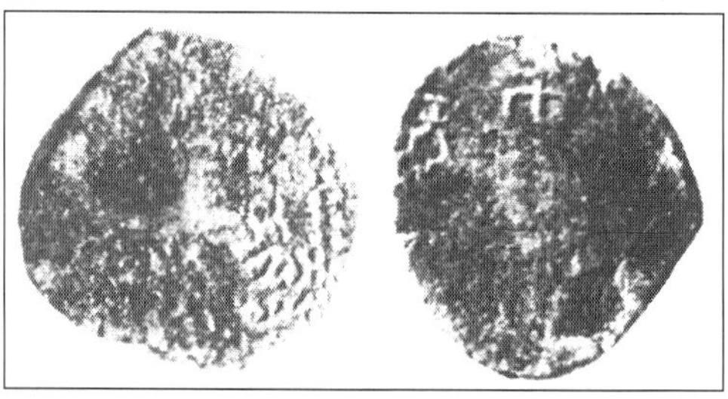

Copper, irregularly round, 10.195 g, 23 x 25 mm

Obv.: Device totally effaced. In the upper portion, part of the legend (*to chitreśvara*), all within double-beaded border.

Rev.: Deer standing to left in front of parasoled six-arched hill symbol, *svastika* on the back of the deer.

Ref.: Shastri 1984: p. 26, no. 4.

Var. 2

Obv.: Tri-cephalous Śiva seated on Apasmāra-purusha with right hand raised and left resting on left knee, trident on left and female figure on right, traces of Brāhmī letters on 3 – 4 o'clock position.

Rev.: Deer to left with *svastika* and star-like symbol on back in a deep die impression.

Ref.: BM, Acc. No. 1985-4-26-4, 2.1 x 2.65 cm, 10.596 g (Handa 2007, Pl. LXXXIV.1).

Var. 3

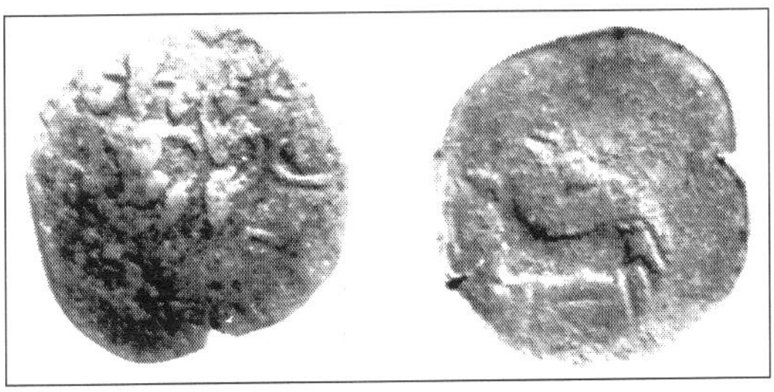

Obv.: Three-headed Śiva as above bearing heavy *jaṭābhāra*, female figure wearing an *ekāvali* 'pearl necklace' and dhoti up to the knees standing slightly turned towards him with right hand raised and left suspended downwards touching the shanks, traces of the legend (- *-vata-chatr*—) along the right edge from about 12.30 to 3.0 o'clock position indicating the legend to have begun at about 10 o'clock position and continuing to about 9 o'clock with a gap between 5 and 7 o'clock (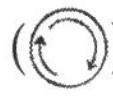).

Rev.: Deer to left with traces of square vase with parasol and another symbol above and *Indradhvaja* below.
Ref.: British Museum, Acc. No. 1983 (1), Tye-79, 2.2 x 2.4 cm, 10.743 g (Handa 2007, Pl. LXXXII.3).

Var. 4

Obv.: Tri-cephalous Śiva seated on Apasmāra-purusha with female figure on his left standing in profile looking at him.
Rev.: Deer to left with *śrīvatsa* in horns and parasoled square box on back facing a female standing cross-legged, holding the long shaft of lance or trident in her left hand, square box with parasol on the back of deer, dotted border around.
Ref.: Garhwal Hoard (Negative no. 378/1-17, card no. 17).

Var. 5

Obv.: Śiva seated on Apasmāra-purusha.
Rev.: Deer to left with hollow square box with parasol on the back.
Ref.: Maheshwari collection (10.41 g, 24 x 23 mm).

Var. 6

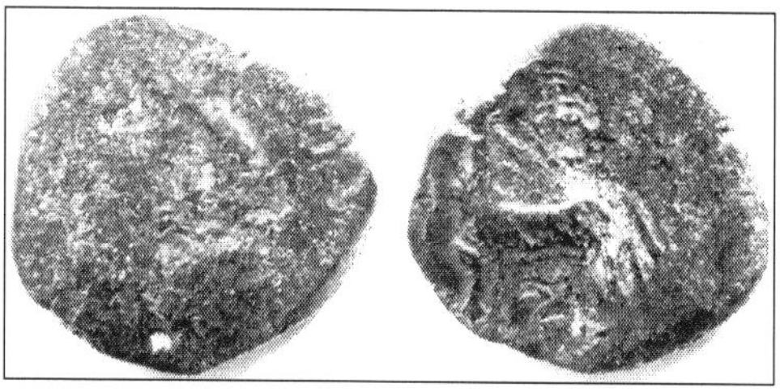

Obv.: Traces of Śiva seated on Apasmāra-purusha.
Rev.: Deer to left with hollow box having multiple parasols above and dumb-bell below.
Ref.: Maheshwari collection (10.91 g, 23 mm).

Var. 7

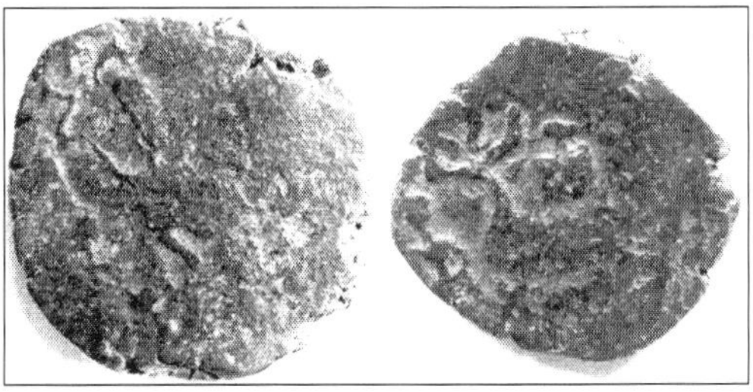

Obv.: Tri-cephalous Śiva seated on Apasmāra-purusha.
Rev.: Deer to left with *śrīvatsa* in horns and solid square box with parasol on back facing a female depicted slantingly with left hand on hip.
Ref.: Maheshwari collection (9.12 g, 22 x 21 mm).

Var. 8

Obv.: Śiva seated on Apasmāra-purusha as usual, traces of - - - *mahātmanaḥ* between 7 and 10 o'clock position indicating that the legend began at about 1 or 2 o'clock position.
Rev.: Deer to left facing arched *chaitya* with square box on back and dumb-bell below , border of dots.
Ref.: Garhwal Hoard: Negative no. 378/2-22, card no. 46.

Var. 9

Obv.: Traces of the god with right hand raised, twisted shaft and bold letters - - tochitr—on left.

Rev.: Deer to left facing female deity with left hand on hip, dumb-bell () below the deer.

Ref.: Garhwal Hoard: Negative no. 382/3-6, card no. 317, 10-585 g, 21 x 13 mm.

Another coin in this hoard (Negative no. 382/3-2, card no. 313, 9.885 g, 22 x 20 mm) seems to have been similar but preserves a solid square box above the back of the deer –

Var. 10

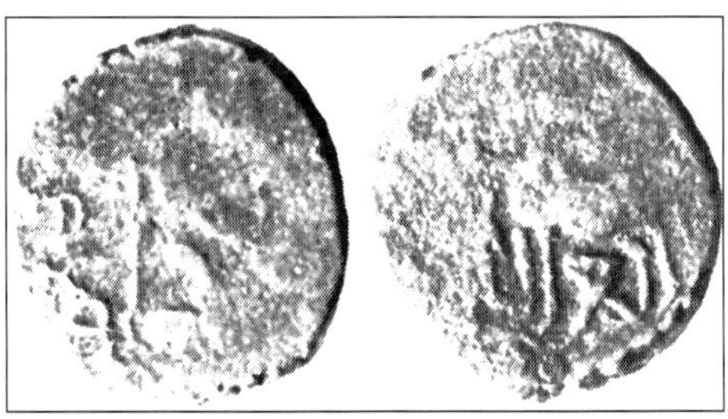

Obv.: Śiva as usual, *-gavata cha-* from 7 to 9 o'clock position indicating that the legend began at 4 or 5 o'clock position.

Rev.: Deer facing left, traces of female figure on left, dumb-bell under the deer, beaded border.

Ref.: Garhwal Hoard: Negative no. 382/3-6, 2.1 cm, 10.770 g, card no. 316.

Var. 11

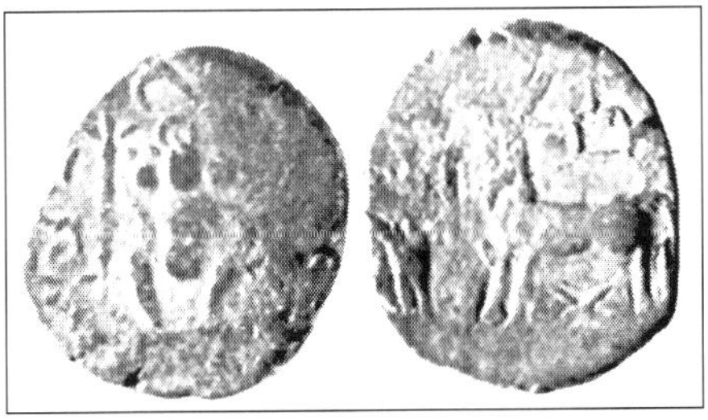

Obv.: Śiva seated on Apasmāra-purusha bearing circular *jaṭābhāra* holding trident with outward flaring spikes in his right hand, *Bha* at 11 o'clock and *mahātmanaḥ* between 7 and 10 o'clock indicating the legend beginning between 11 to 10 o'clock position (), side heads too are circular and the left one seems to have two dots above indicating top-knots.

Rev.: deer facing female on left, square box above and dumb-bell below the animal.

Ref.: Garhwal Hoard: Negative no. 378/1-15, card no. 15.

A coin of this variety (INHCRF-1310.31 g, 23 x 23 mm) shows the legend Chitresva(ra) between 1 and 4 o' clock indicating the similar disposition of the legend. It has the female figure standing to the left of the god on the obverse as much better preserved with bold dots around. The reverse shows the deer to left with linear square box having a parasol above and dumb-bell below –

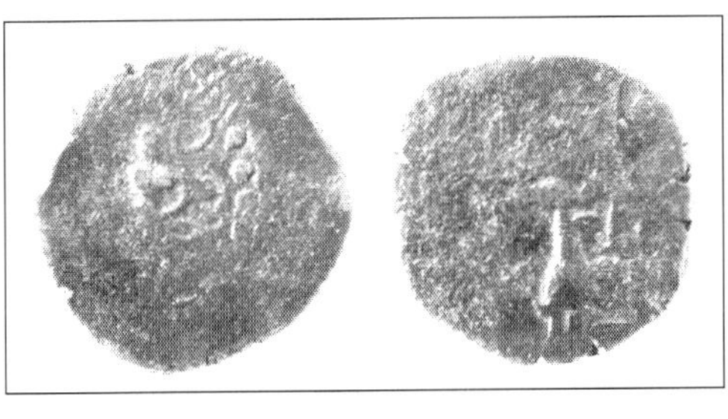

Var. 12

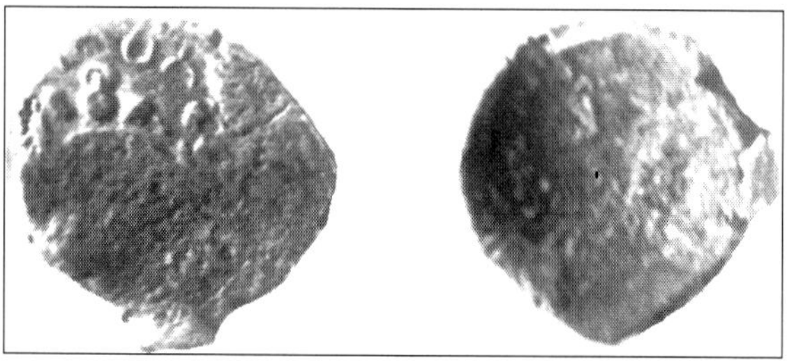

Obv: Śiva as above but with circular *jaṭābhāra* on central head slightly different from the preceding one, *gavata* from about 12 to 1 o'clock position indicating the beginning of the legend from 10 o'clock position, traces of female figure on Śiva's left.
Rev: Completely effaced.
Ref.: Garhwal Hoard: Negative no. 378/2-23, card no. 47.

Var. 13

Obv.: Tri-cephalous Śiva seated on Apasmāra-purusha as usual with female figure on his left, *triratna* symbol between them.
Rev.: Deer facing female figure standing to front on left with her right hand raised to the level of the shoulder and left akimbo, dots around.
Ref.: Garhwal Hoard: Negative no. 378/2-11, card no. 35.

Var. 14

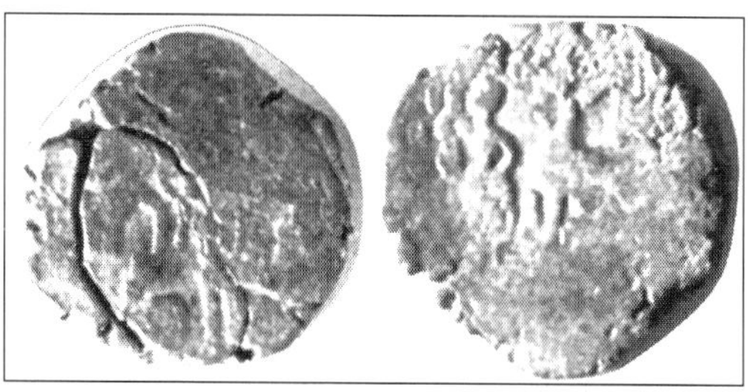

Obv.: Śiva as usual with female figure standing to front on his left (three cracked pieces joined together).

Rev.: As above, the female figure seems to hold an object (lotus?) in her right hand and the deer has a square vase on its back, beaded border.

Ref.: Garhwal Hoard: Negative no. 378/1-11, card no. 11.

Var. 15

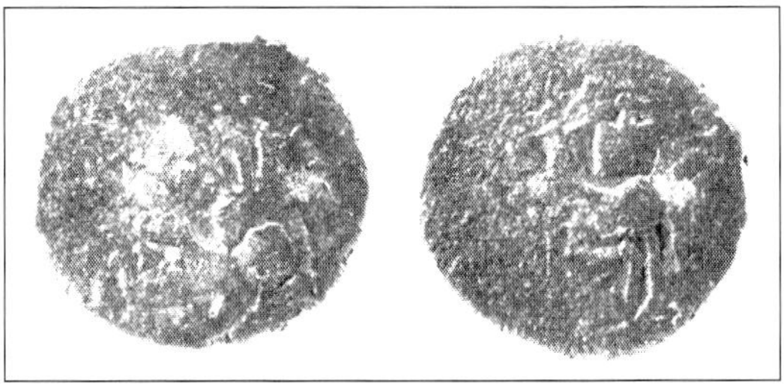

Obv.: Śiva as usual but the female figure on right seems to be standing on a square pedestal with a big round block on it.

Rev.: Deer to left with solid square box with parasol on its back and dumb-bell below.

Ref.: INHCRF-8, 10.83 g, 24 x 24 mm.

Var. 16

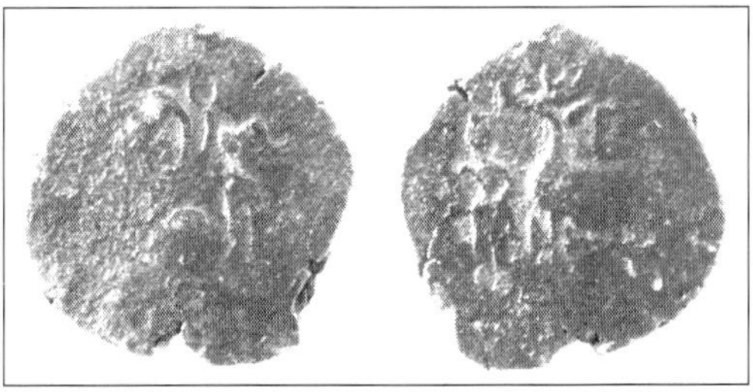

Obv.: Śiva as usual but the female figure on his left standing facing is holding linear round object (lotus?) in her upraised right hand.

Rev.: Deer to left facing a female figure with right hand raised and left hand on hip and free end of the sari suspended, hollow square box with parasol above the back of the deer, object below not clear.

Ref.: INHCRF-6, 9.54 g, 20 x 24 mm.

Var. 17

Obv.: Śiva as usual seated on Apasmāra-purusha holding inverted trident in his right hand with spikes below with traces of female on his left.

Rev.: Deer to left facing an elongated enface female figure wearing *sari* standing with feet turned sideways at right angles having upraised right hand holding the lotus stalk and left hand suspended, beaded border around.

Ref.: INHCRF-1, 10.20 g, 23 x 24 mm.

Var. 18

Obv.: Śiva as usual.

Rev.: Deer to left, female figure on left effaced, solid square box on the back of deer and triangle-headed symbol below.

Ref.: Maheshwari collection (11.0 g, 22 x 19 mm).

Var. 19

Obv.: As above.
Rev.: As above but square box below the deer.
Ref.: Maheshwari collection (8.68 g, 20 x 21 mm).

Type II: Tri-cephalous Chitreśvara/Deer to Right

As referred to above, three of the four coins described by Prof. Shastri showed the deer to right. They represent the following varieties.

Var. 1

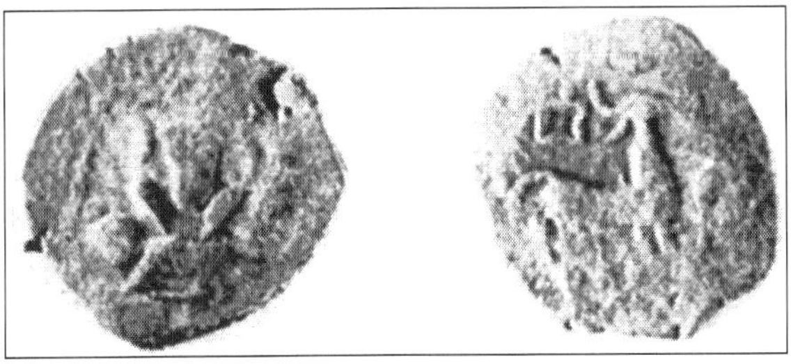

Obv.: God Śiva holding a trident-axe (club according to Shastri) and left placed on knee, with raised right hand seated with feet resting on the back of a kneeling figure (identified as Apasmāra-purusha) with traces of human figure on right.
Rev.: Deer standing facing right with traces of a human figure in front, a square bodied vase (*kalaśa*) on the back of the deer, the symbol below the deer is not clear.
Ref.: Shastri 1984: p. 25, no. 1: 2.0 x 2.2 cm, 8.625 g.

INHCRF possesses a similar coin (Negative no. 615/1-1) which shows dumb-bell below the deer very clearly-

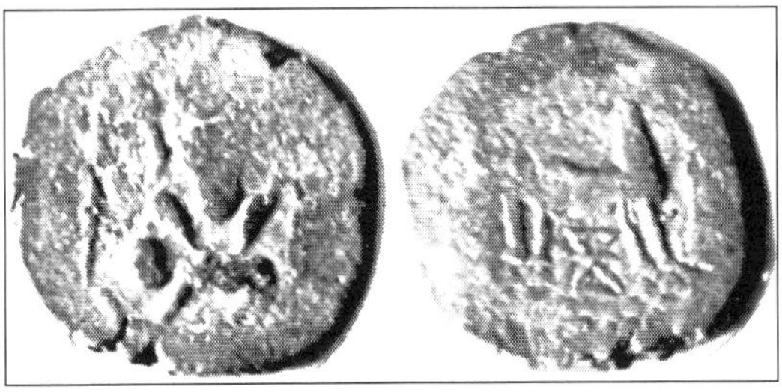

Similar obverse and deer to right having square hollow box or vase with parasol on its back and dumb-bell below facing the female are, however, clear on another specimen –

Ref.: INHCRF-9, 10.84 g, 20 x 23 mm

That the female figure in front of the deer to right on the reverse of such coins stood to front with right hand raised and left akimbo with feet splayed sideways in a border of dots may be discerned on another coin of this variety –

Ref.: INHCRF-7, 9.89 g, 20 x 24 mm

Var. 2

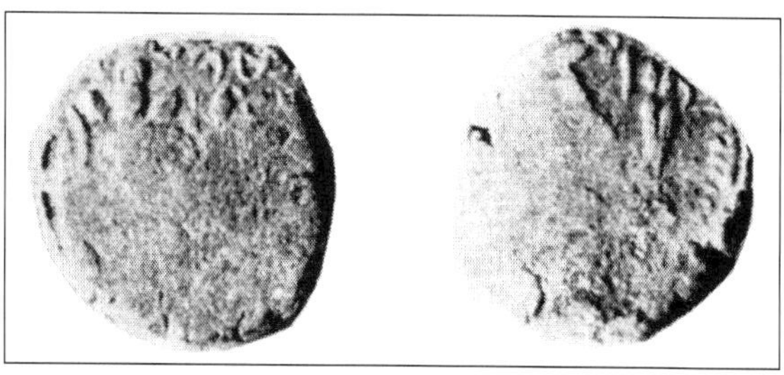

Obv.: Tri-cephalous Śiva bearing circular locks of hair, holding a trident with visible right prong curved, upper portion of human figure on right holding some indistinct object (lotus?) in right hand, Brāhmī letters on the upper edge reads *vata chatra* and seems to start at about 10–11 o'clock.

Rev.: Deer to right facing female, traces of beaded border.

Ref.: Shastri 1984: pp. 25-26, no. 2: 2.2 cm, 9.600 g.

Var. 3

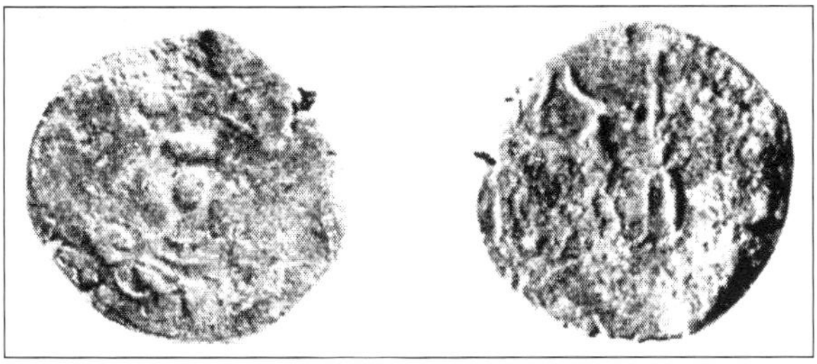

Obv.: Śiva as above with female on his left.
Rev.: Deer to right facing a linear figure holding a spear-like object with right hand resting the left on hip.
Ref.: *Ibid*, p. 26, no. 3: 2.1 cm, 8.540 g.

Var. 4

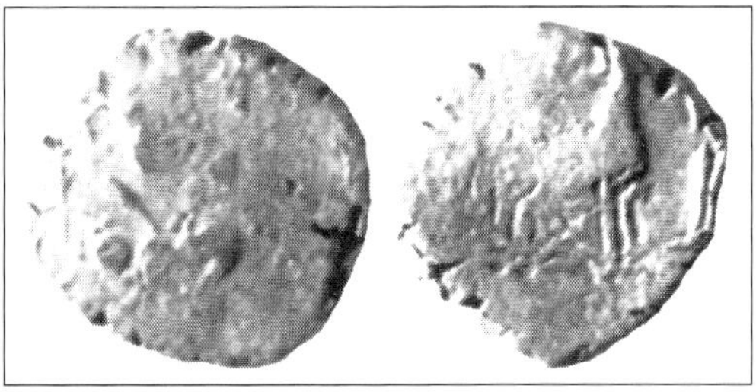

Obv.: Tri-cephalous Śiva seated on Apasmāra-purusha as usual, trident of a different type on left.
Rev.: Deer to right with a dumb-bell below, female below waist on right slightly turned towards the deer.
Ref.: Garhwal Hoard: Negative no. 378/2-18, card no. 42.

Var. 5

Obv.: Śiva on Apasmāra as usual with traces on female on right.
Rev.: Deer to right with dumb-bell (⧗) below, female figure on right with right hand raised and left akimbo.
Ref.: Garhwal Hoard: Negative no. 378/1-8, card no. 5.

Another coin of this variety in the same hoard (Negative no. 378/1-14, card no. 14) shows the flaring spikes of the trident in Śiva's right hand on the obverse and border of dots on the reverse clearly though the dumb-bell under the deer is visible only in traces -

Var. 6

Obv.: Similar but the Apasmāra-purusha seems to have turned his face to his left in three-quarters profile and the god holds the slantingly placed weapon.
Rev.: As above with clearly depicted dumb-bell under the deer.
Ref.: INHCRF-12, 9.05 g, 21 x 22 mm.

Var. 7

Obv.: As on Var. 5 but the legs of the deer don't show any incline and there are traces of the legend along the right edge.
Rev.: Similar but female figure is inclined at about 45 degrees.
Ref.: INHCRF-4, 8.86 g, 23 x 23 mm.

Var. 7

Obv.: As above but the shaft of the weapon seems to be barbed.
Rev.: Deer to right with longish face facing the female deity whose right hand is rising almost vertically, vase on the back of the deer and dumb-bell below.
Ref.: Maheshwari collection (11-16 g, 21 x 23 mm).

Var. 8

Obv.: As above but Śiva with central head bearing circular *jaṭābhāra* and side heads crested, female on right with right hand raised.
Rev.: As above, deer with twisted short tail to right with vase above and dumb-bell below.
Ref.: Garhwal Hoard: Negative no. 378/2-6, card no. 30.

Some coins in Maheshwari collection are also similar though the devices are not very clear –

(9.70 g, 23 mm)

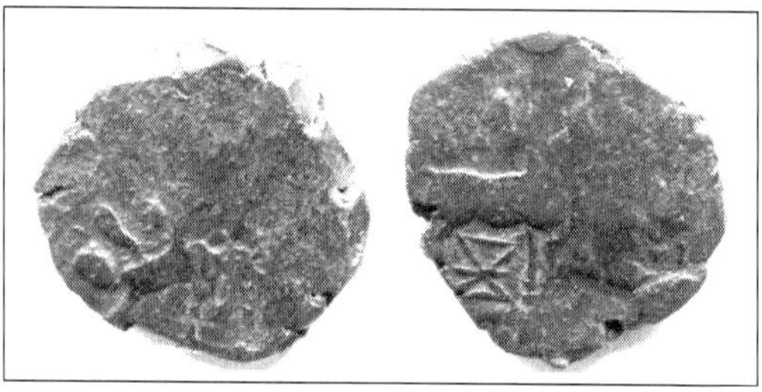

(10.05 g, 21 x 22 mm)

There seems to be a symbol (vase?) above the deer.

(9.64 g, 21 mm)

The obverse is better preserved and the reverse shows traces of dotted border also.

Var. 9

Obv.: Śiva as usual but the trident has a long curved shaft of pellets with flaring spikes.

Rev.: Deer to right with dumb-bell (X) below, almost complete figure of female on right with right hand raised and left akimbo, wearing nether garment and feet held sideways, dotted border.

Ref.: Garhwal Hoard: Negative no. 378/1-18, card no. 18.

Var. 10

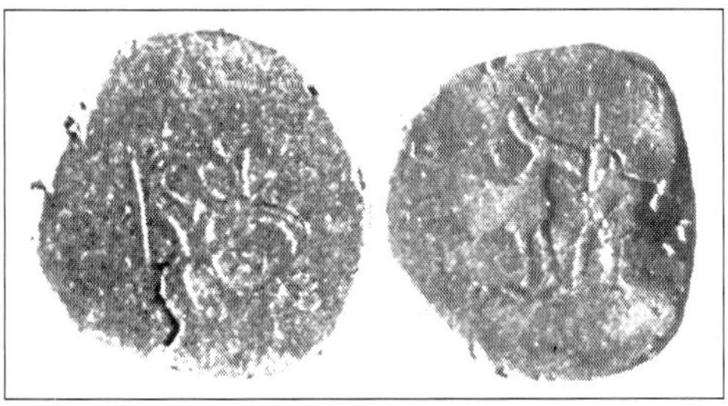

Obv.: Slightly obese figure of three-headed Śiva holding the shaft of the trident-axe in his right hand with left on corresponding knee, traces of dotted border.

Rev.: Ass-like figure of the deer to right with dumb-bell under it, female on right wearing sari and holding the long shaft of a lance in right hand with left on hip, traces of dotted border.

Ref.: Garhwal Hoard: Negative no. 378/1-12, card no. 12.

Var. 11

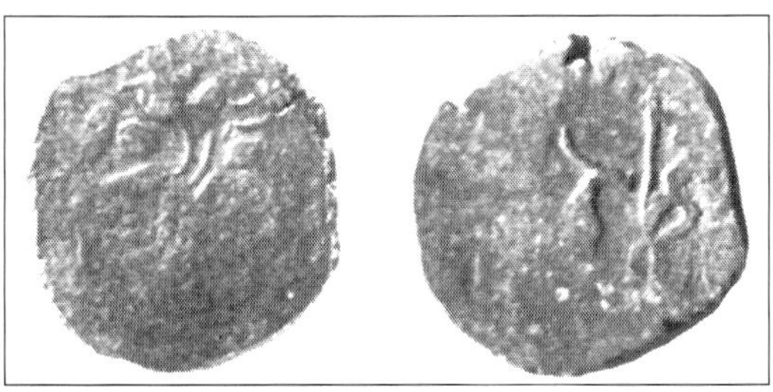

Obv.: Śiva as usual with traces of female on right holding lotus by its stalk in her right hand.

Rev.: Deer to right facing a female figure bending backwards holding a straight vertical spear in right hand resting the left on hip, beaded border.

Ref.: Garhwal Hoard: Negative no. 378/1-19, card no. 19.

Var. 12

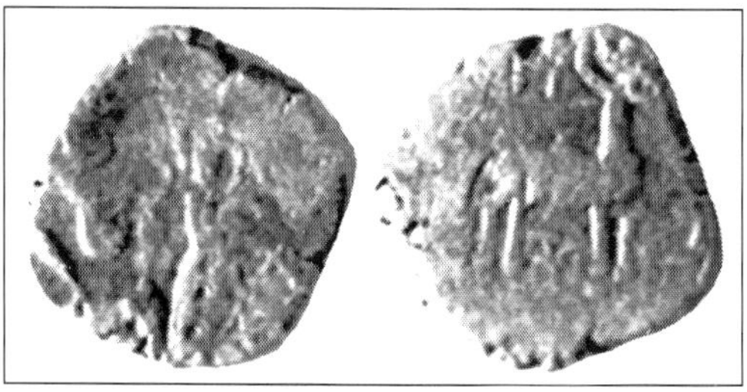

Obv.: Śiva with female on right as usual, traces of legend along right edge.

Rev.: Deer to right with square vase above and *Indradhvaja* below.

Ref.: Garhwal Hoard: Negative no. 378/2-10, card no. 34.

Var. 13

Obv.: Traces of the usual devices but female depicted with a skirt within border of dots, edge cracked.

Rev.: Deer to right with vase above and *Indradhvaja* () below.

Ref.: Garhwal Hoard: Negative no. 378/2-5, card no. 29.

Var. 14

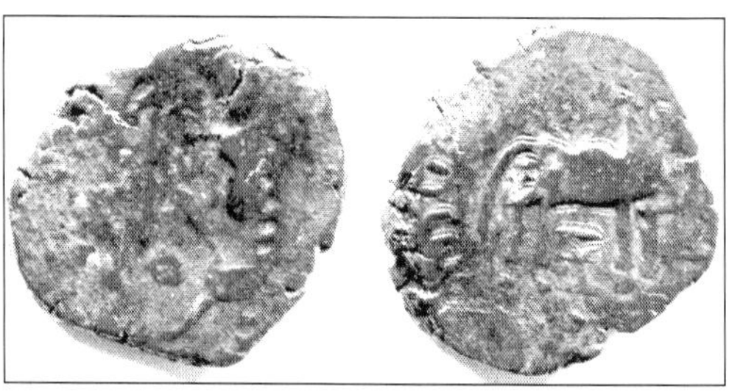

Obv.: Double impression of the god seated on kneeling figure because of die-shift, beaded border.
Rev.: Deer to right with triangle-headed standard below, rayed line border visible on left edge.
Ref.: Maheshwari collection (9.81 g, 20 x 22 mm).

Var. 15

Obv.: Tri-cephalous Śiva seated on Apasmāra as usual, female on right standing enface with heels touching each other but feet splayed outwards, wearing sari, hands as usual, traces of legend on right.
Rev.: Deer to right with *Indradhvaja* (Ÿ) below.
Ref.: Garhwal Hoard: Negative no. 380/1-9, card no. 153.

Var. 16

Obv.: As above only in traces.
Rev.: Deer to right with *Indradhvaja* below facing the female deity standing facing with right hand raised and left akimbo, border of rays instead of dots as clearly visible on right edge.
Ref.: Maheshwari collection (10.30 g, 22 x 24 mm).

Var. 17

Obv.: Tri-cephalous Śiva seated on Apasmāra as usual but there seems to be a pedestal below Apasmāra and traces of female figure and legend on right.

Rev.: Deer to right with square vase above and *Indradhvaja* below, traces of female figure on right.

Ref.: INHCRF-2, 10.90 g, 23 x 23 mm.

Var. 18

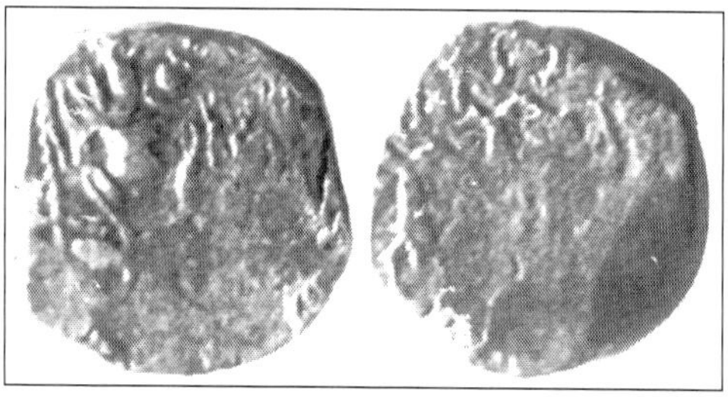

Obv.: Śiva seated on Apasmāra as usual with elaborate locks on central head and three dot-like topknots on his left head and quiver-like object substituting his right side head, holding twisted shaft of the trident in his right hand, female figure on his left slightly turned towards him standing as usual with right hand raised and holding the lotus and left hand resting on hip, traces of dotted border.

Rev.: Deer to right with *śrīvatsa* between horns and traces of female on right, die-shift has left the impression of another deer head on left.

Ref.: Garhwal Hoard: Negative no. 378/1-22, card no. 22.

Var. 19

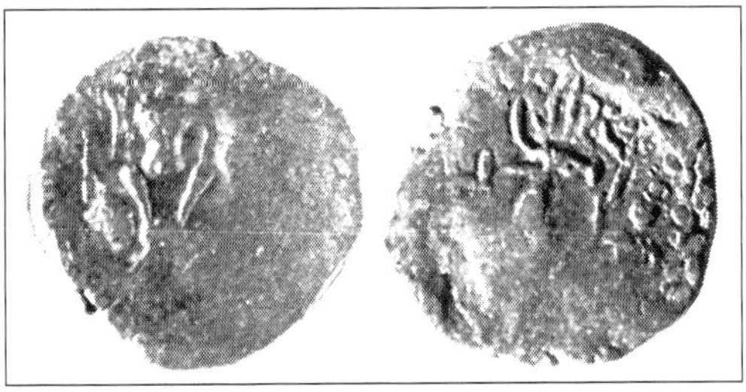

Obv.: Śiva as usual with trident on his right and traces of female figure holding lotus in right hand on right.

Rev.: Deer to right with square vase on back, *śrīvatsa* between horns (), female figure on right holding big lotus in right hand held above the head, left hand on hip, topknot held in position by bead string, beaded border.

Ref.: Garhwal Hoard: Negative no. 378/1-16, card no. 10.

Var. 20

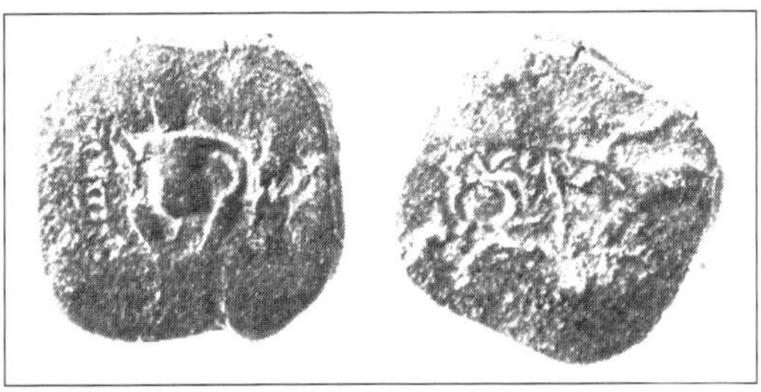

Obv.: Śiva as usual with trident on his right having triangular base and serration marks on the shaft, female figure as usual on his left.

Rev.: Deer to right with a different type of *pūrṇa-kalaśa* 'full vase' and a barbed arrow upwards on its back.

Ref.: INHCRF-3, 10.12 g, 20 x 21 mm.

Var. 21

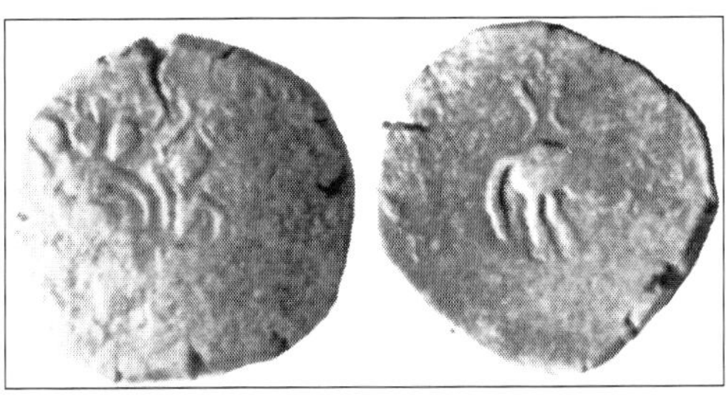

Obv.: Traces of Śiva and female as usual but Śiva's central head has a round topknot.

Rev.: Hind part of deer to right with a different type of *śrīvatsa* ( ) above its back, traces of the legend *mahātmana* from 7 to 10 o'clock position.

Ref.: Garhwal Hoard: Negative no. 378/1-9, card no. 8.

Var. 22

Obv.: As usual.

Rev.: As usual but *śrīvatsa* or nāga symbol ( ) above the back of the deer and dumb-bell below it.

Ref.: Garhwal Hoard: 7.780 g, 20 mm, card no. 1/25.

(Numerous coins in the hoard show the *nāga* symbol ( ) above the back of the deer: card no. 1/10, 9.265 g, 22 mm; card nos. 728, 765, etc.)

Var. 23

Obv.: Śiva seated on Apasmāra with upper part out of flan and female figure on right.

Rev.: Deer to right with *svastika* above and dumb-bell ( ) below, border of dots.

Ref.: Garhwal Hoard: Negative no. 378/2-8, card no. 27.

Var. 22

Obv.: Similar but healthier god with heads intact and flaring spikes of the trident clearly visible.
Rev.: Similar but tail of deer closer to hind legs.
Ref.: Garhwal Hoard: Negative no. 378/3-7, card no. 85.

Var. 23

Obv.: Śiva seated on Apasmāra as usual.
Rev.: Deer to right with *triratna* above the head and *svastika* above the back.
Ref.: Garhwal Hoard: card no. 749.

Var. 24

Obv.: Apasmāra-purusha to left lying supine resting his body on elbows and knees, traces of trident on left and a symbol or letter looking like *svastika* below.
Rev.: Deer to right with square vase above.
Ref.: Garhwal Hoard: Negative no. 378/2-17, card no. 41.

Var. 25

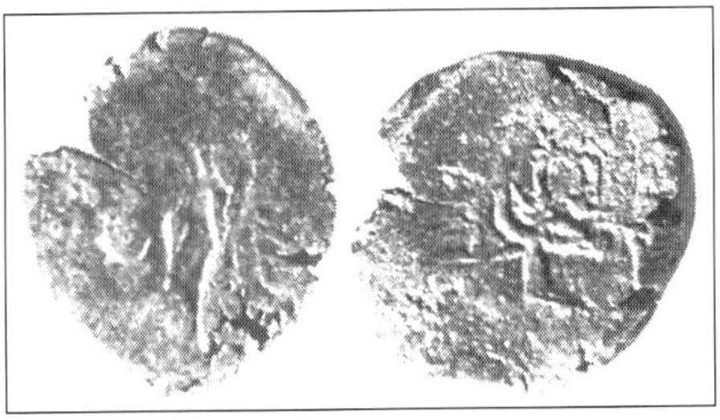

Obv.: Śiva as usual, female on right standing turned towards the god, traces of Brāhmī letters along the right edge.
Rev.: Deer to right with elongated pointed face, traces of female on right, inverted vase like symbol above the back of deer.
Ref.: Garhwal Hoard: Negative no. 378/1-4, card no. 4.

Var. 26

Obv.: Partially visible Śiva as usual with female figure on right with right hand rising above slantingly, pleat of hair falling back on her head, traces of legend on right.

Rev.: Deer facing female on right, square vase above the back of deer and dumb-bell below.

Ref.: Garhwal Hoard: Negative no. 378/1-13, card no. 13.

Var. 27

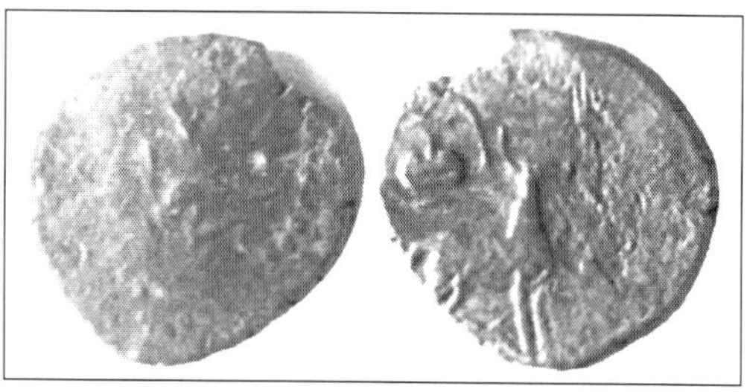

Obv.: Partially visible impression of Śiva as usual, garland-like dotted border.

Rev.: Deer to right having a vase with foliage () on back and dumb-bell below.

Ref.: Garhwal Hoard: Negative no. 378/2-15, card no. 39.

Var. 28

Obv.: Obliterated.

Rev.: Deer to right facing female figure, full vase on pedestal () above and dumb-bell below the deer.

Ref.: Garhwal Hoard: 2.2 cm, 10.950 g, card no. 24.

Var. 29

Obv.: As usual but badly obliterated.
Rev.: Deer to right with *Indradhvaja* below and a very beautiful vase above showing a leaf on a stem coming out of it.
Ref.: Garhwal Hoard: card no. 1/22, 10.550 g, 22 x 21 mm.

Var. 30

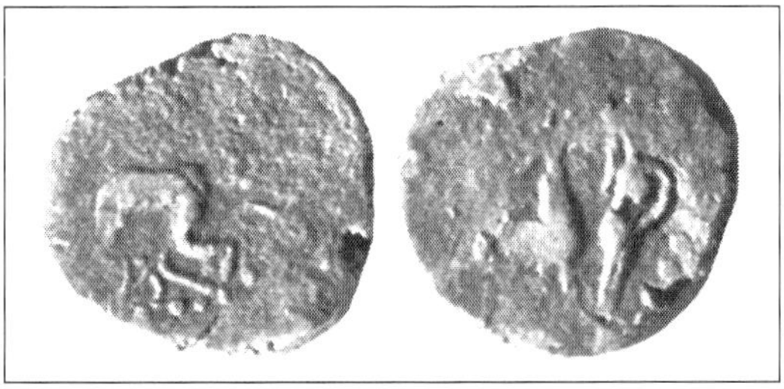

Obv.: Only Apasmāra-purusha visible but with a different posture of legs, some symbol or letter below, dotted border.
Rev.: Deer to right facing female who seems to be turning away but looking at the deer with face turned backwards, her right hand is raised above in the posture of holding lotus stalk and left hand rests on waist, border of dots around.
Ref.: Garhwal Hoard: Negative no. 378/2-2, card no. 26.

Var. 31

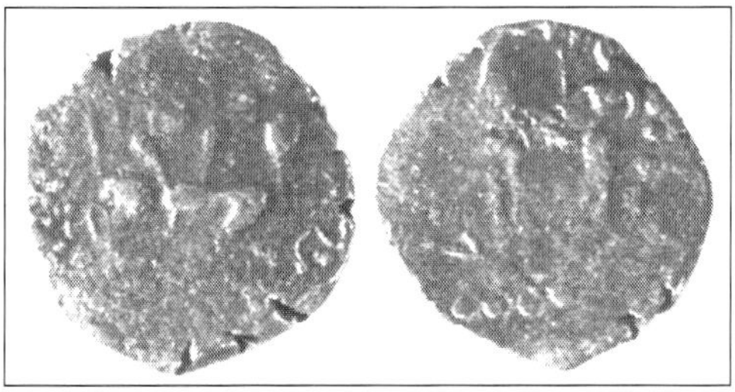

Obv.: Śiva seated on Apasmāra as usual, female on right, *ta chi* at 3–4 o'clock position indicating that the legend began at 1 o'clock position.
Rev.: Deer to right facing female figure turned slightly to her right with left hand on hip and right hand raised to hold the stalk of the lotus, dumb-bell between the legs of the deer, border of big dots.
Ref.: Garhwal Hoard: Negative no. 378/2-4, card no. 28.

Var. 32

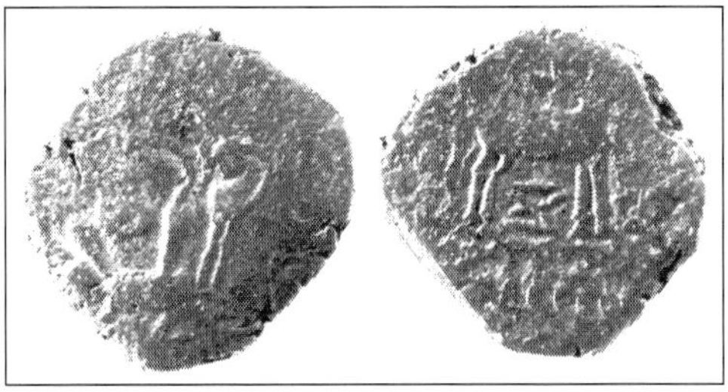

Obv.: As above but the female stands in *dvi-bhaṅga* 'double flexion pose' with her waist swayed to her left and bust inclined towards the god.

Rev.: Deer to right with vase (?) above and dumb-bell below, serrated border.

Ref.: INHCRF-10, 11.15 g, 24 x 23 mm.

Var. 32

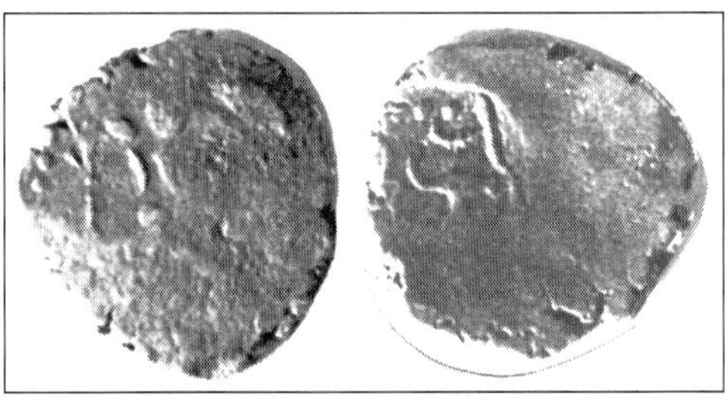

Obv.: Partially impressed device showing Śiva seated on Apasmāra as usual with right hand held upwards, trident with pelleted shaft on left, border of dots.

Rev.: Forepart of deer to right with traces of female on right with her right hand raised above and dotted crescent with a dot above representing the lotus above the head of the deer ().

Ref.: Garhwal Hoard: Negative no. 379/1-12, card no. 84.

Var. 33

Obv.: Śiva seated on Apasmāra as usual but circular *jaṭābhāra* with a dot in the centre above the central head and *bhagava* on top.

Rev.: As usual but deer to right has an inverted *triratna* above the head and vase above the back, a human figure standing cross-legged wearing *ardhoruk* holding the long stalk of a lotus looking like a spear in right hand, lined border around.

Ref.: Garhwal Hoard: card no. 1/2, 11.010 g, 22 x 20 mm; card no. 1/5, 10.955 g, 20 x 19 mm; etc.

Var. 34

Obv.: As usual but Śiva bears a crescent with big dot above the central head.

Rev.: Deer having a vase above standing to right facing a peaked hill from which emanates at its top a bent line with a *svastika* on the right hand side.

Ref.: Garhwal Hoard: card no. 1/12, 8.790 g, 22 x 19 mm.

The British Museum purchased coins of this type in the eighties of the last century, in all probability belonging to the hoard a substantial part of which was acquired by the Birla Archaeological and Cultural Research Institute, Hyderabad. The details of type, sizes and weights of the coins are given below.

Acc. No. 1983(1) TYE-77, 2.1 x 2.35 cm, 11.181 g (Handa 2007, Pl. LXXXII.1)
Acc. No. 1983(1) TYE-78, 2.15 cm, 10.718 g (*Ibid*, Pl. LXXXII.2)
Acc. No. 1983(1) TYE-80, 1.95 x 2.5 cm, 10.062 g (*Ibid*, Pl. LXXXIII.1)
Acc. No. 1983(1) TYE-81, 1.9 x 2.3 cm, 8.935 g (*Ibid*, Pl. LXXXIII.2
Acc. No. 1983(1) TYE-82, 1.9 x 2.3 cm, 11.266 g) (*Ibid*, LXXXIII.3)
Acc. No. 1983-6-2-2, 2.45 x 2.3 cm, 10.845 g
Acc. No. 1985-4-26-5, 2.25 x 2.45 cm, 9.322 g (*Ibid*, Pl. LXXXIV.2)
Acc. No. 1985-4-26-6, 2.0 x 2.4 cm, 10.582 g (*Ibid*, Pl. LXXXIV.3)
Three of these coins present new varieties.

Var. 35

Obv.: As above.
Rev.: Deer to right facing the female, bold *śrīvatsa* between the horns,  on its back and *Indradhvaja* below between the legs.
Ref.: BM, Acc. No. 1985-4-26-6, 2.0 x 2.4 cm, 10.582 g.

Var. 36

Obv.: As above but having a dotted vertical shaft of the weapon to his right, the central head of the god indicates what Prof. Shastri had guessed to be Gaṅgā flowing from the locks.
Rev.: Deer to right having *Indradhvaja* between legs facing slantingly placed female.
Ref.: BM, Acc. No. 1983(1), Tye-79, 2.2 x 2.4 cm, 10.743 g.

Var. 37

Obv.: Tri-cephalous Śiva seated on Apasmāra, female figure on right turned towards the god with right hand raised and left on waist, die shift has left double impression of the border of dots visible between 3 and 6 o' clock position. Jargoned legend may be seen from 12 to 5 o'clock indicating the beginning of the legend at about 10 o'clock position (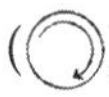), border of dots.
Rev.: Deer to right with unidentifiable symbol (*śrīvatsa*?) over head, square vase above and *Indradhvaja* below, border of dots.

Var. 38

Obv.: Partially visible device of the god as above with female figure on right and partial legend *Maha(tmana)* along the right edge, betraying the disposition of the legend as starting from about 7 o'clock position and ending at about 5 o'clock position with perhaps a gap between 11 and 2 o'clock (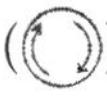), all within beaded border.

Rev.: Deer to right with linear square box capped by a parasol, rest worn out and obliterated.

Ref.: INHCRF (Negative no. 614/1-11).

Var. 39

Obv.: Similar but only the twisted lower portion of the weapon is visible and the legend has survived only in traces.

Rev.: Similar but the female figure on the right is depicted as at about 45 degrees.

Ref.: Pieper 2013: pp. 378-79, 9.67 g, 20 mm.

Pieper's coin too comes from Monica Tye [ex-list 10 (1994), no. 330] like the British Museum coins and may have originally belonged to the Garhwal Hoard. A coin of this type and variety in the Garhwal

Hoard (Negative no. 378/2-21, card no. 145), though badly worn out, shows the legend beginning at 10 o'clock on the obverse (◎). The reverse shows almost a linear figure of the goddess standing holding a lotus stalk in her right hand with left akimbo:

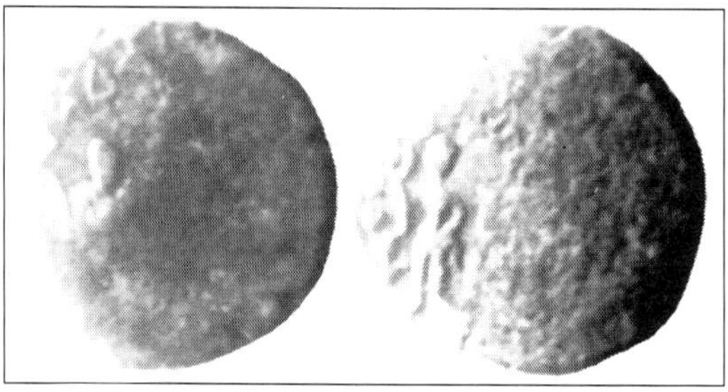

Var. 40

Obv.: As usual but only the kneeling figure to left with lower legs of the god visible, beaded border around.

Rev.: Deer to right with traces of square vase above and triangle-headed symbol below, female figure on right inclined at 45 degrees seems to be standing cross-legged.

Ref.: INHCRF-5, 10.28 g, 23 x 22 mm.

There are numerous coins in the Garhwal Hoard which cannot be classified properly. That individual collections too may have such examples may be demonstrated by an example which though showing the usual devices almost clearly pose the difficulty of definite classification –

Maheshwari collection (8.23 g, 20 x 22 mm)

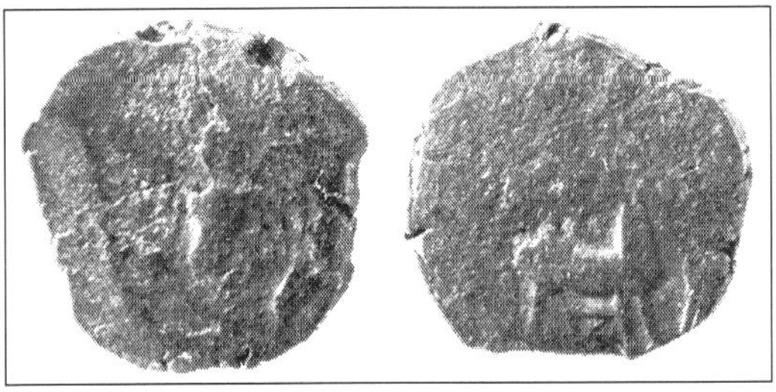

INHCRF-11, 9.32 g, 22 x 21 mm

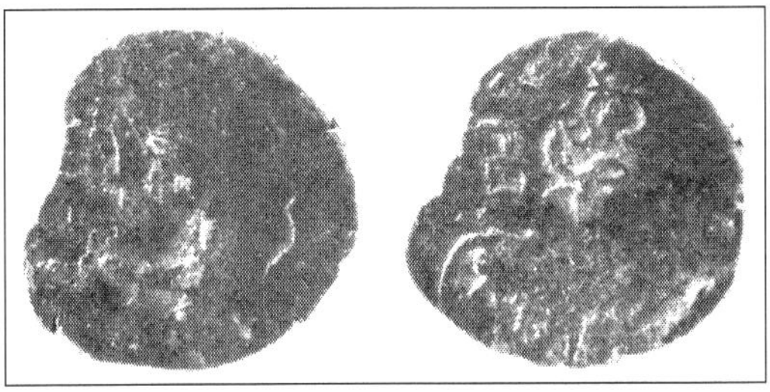

INHCRF-15, 9.61 g, 21 x 23 mm

INCHRF (Negative no. 379/1-20)

CLASS C: INDETERMINATE DEITY TYPE

Type I

Var. 1

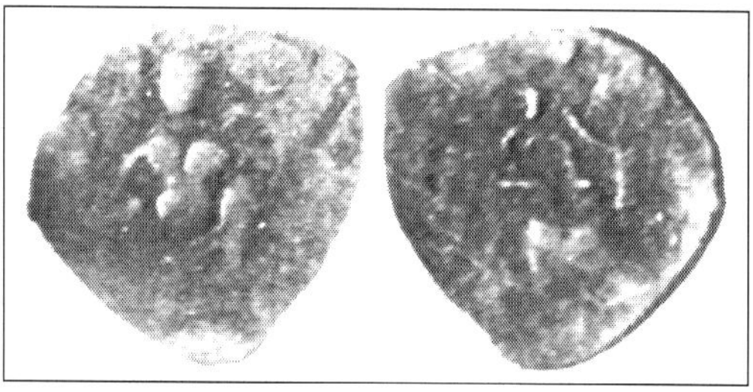

Obv.: Mono-cephalous muscular figure (Śiva looking like a goddess seated on Apasmāra-purusha?).

Rev.: Deer to right with a queer vase or symbol () above its back.

Ref.: Garhwal Hoard: Negative no. 378/1-24, card no. 24.

Var. 2

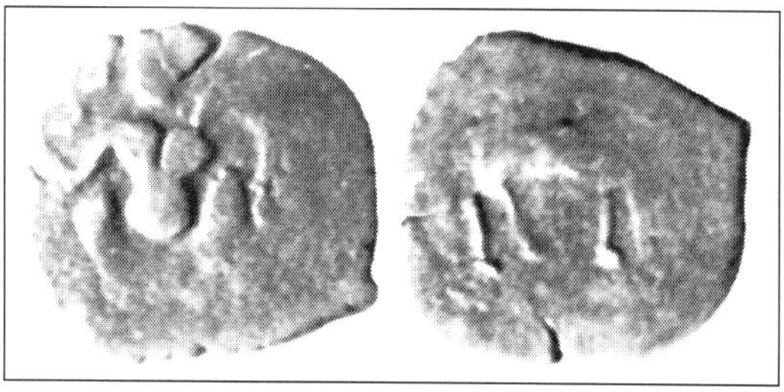

Obv.: As above but face seems to be turned slightly towards proper right and perhaps holding a water pot in left hand.

Rev.: Deer to right, traces of *Indradhvaja* below, border of dots.

Ref.: Garhwal Hoard: Negative no. 378/2-1, card no. 25.

Both of these two coins are of thin fabric different from others. Only better preserved specimens in future will determine whether the deity is male or female and seated on Apasmāra-purusha or not.

3

The Devices and Iconographic Importance

As noted above, all the coins of Garhwal Hoard betray very poor craftsmanship and quality, much reduced from the Kuṇinda coins of Amoghabhūti and the copper/potin Bull/Elephant (*Yaudheyānāṃ Bahudhāñake*) type coins of the Yaudheyas (Allan's Class 2) and the Brahmaṇyadeva type single silver and numerous copper coins (Allan's Class 3 type Yaudheya coins). Like their Yaudheya counterparts of Allan's Class 3 the production of most of Chitreśvara type coins appears so idiosyncratic that every coin seems to form its own type. A look at the illustrations reveals that most of the devices on the coins of the hoard have either been only partially accommodated or have not come out at all because of defective striking. Numerous pieces in the hoard do not show recognizable devices and legends making it difficult to ascribe them with any definiteness. As such, the discovery of better preserved coins in future may result in merging some of the varieties distinguished here. The deer with *śrīvatsa* between the horns and some subsidiary symbols under and above it on Kārttikeya/Deer (Class 3 Yaudheya) and Chitreśvara type recall the Kuṇinda coin devices of Amoghabhūti to whom are ascribed beautiful Kuṇinda silver, and copper specie of neat fabric with complete legends, course fabric with incomplete legends and some very rare coins with complete legends in two lines (Class I, II and III according to Allan). Allan regarded Chitreśvara as anonymous Kuṇinda coins. He dated Amoghabhūti's coins to the end of the first century BCE and the anonymous Chitreśvara type to about three centuries later. He observed that the module of

Amoghabhūti's silver coins was suggested by the hemidrachms of the later Greek kings though the types are purely Indian. The legends are in Prakrit, in Brāhmī on the obverse and Kharoshṭhī on the reverse. Though Cunningham (ASR, XIV, 188) had referred to copper coins bearing Kharoshṭhī legend also on the reverse, they are quite rare and not represented in the British Museum collection which show the border of dots replacing the Kharoshṭhī legend.

To appreciate the similarities of these different coin-types of Kuṇinda, Kārttikeya- Shashṭhī/Deer and Chitreśvara types let us know the details of the Kuṇinda coins. Their obverse bears a deer to right and a figure of Lakshmī, standing facing on a lotus and holding a lotus in her uplifted right hand. Between the horns of the deer is the cobra or *śrīvatsa* symbol and above its back exists a box-like symbol. Subsidiary symbols sometimes exist under the deer, between the deer and the goddess, under the feet of the goddess and in the legend running around along the edge. The reverse generally shows a multi-arched *chaitya* with parasol above surmounted by *nandipada* or *triratna* symbol, tree in railing on right, *svastika* with *Indradhvaja* under it on left and river line below:

Yaudheya coins of Class 3 have adopted the features of the obverse of Kuṇinda coins but have relegated them to their reverse –

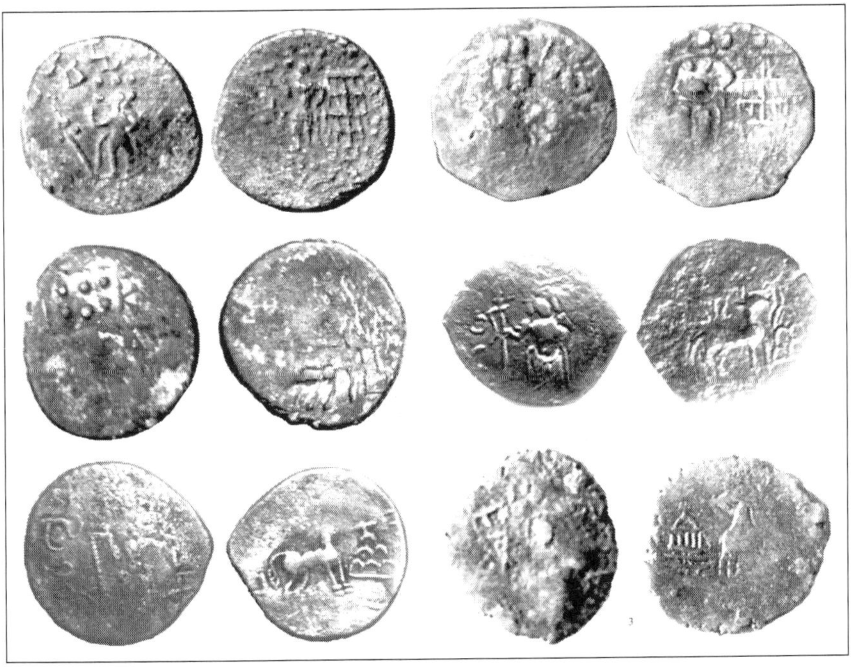

The Chitreśvara type coins substitute the figure of six-headed Kārttikeya with the figure of Śiva standing holding the trident-battleaxe in the right hand with left hand on hip. It is, however, interesting to note that the Yaudheyas too had struck coins showing Śiva holding a trident-battleaxe in the right hand with left akimbo having the legend around on the obverse exactly as shown on single headed Chitreśvara type coins (Handa 2007: Pl. XLIX.1). A similar coin exists in the collection of Jan Lingen (Pieper 2015: p. 49, Fig. 14).

The Kārttikeya-Shashṭhī/Deer type and Chitreśvara coins are much inferior in execution to the Amoghabhūti type coins of the Kuṇindas and Bull/Elephant type Yaudheya coins of Allan's Class 2 betraying political, economic, cultural and technical downfall. The obverse device of Amoghabhūti's coins has been relegated to the reverse of Śiva-Chitreśvara type like those of Kārttikeya/Deer type Yaudheya coins. While the female figure on the obverse standing by the side of tricephalous Śiva has been suggested by Shastri to be an attendant, the female figure on the reverse has not been identified by him. These coins have been found in the big Garhwal hoard comprising only the tri-cephalous Chitreśvara and Shaḍānana/Deer and Shaḍānana/Shashṭhī types. So we feel inclined to regard the female figure on the reverse of tri-cephalous Śiva-Chitreśvara type as the spouse of the god depicted on the obverse, i.e. Pārvatī. The Shaḍānana/Shashṭhī type provides the parallel example.

The weights of most of the available specimens vary between 80 and 96 *rattīs* (9.25 and 11.1 g approximately) and discounting the variation in the price of the metal or its purity, the coins seem to have been struck on one denomination only. The technique of manufacture and workmanship seem to be archaic and rough. The die-cutters were not quite experienced to accommodate the symbols and/or devices in proper depth or relief. Planchets were also not properly heated before being struck and care was not taken to adjust the dies properly. All these facts point to an earlier date for these tri-cephalic Śiva-Chitreśvara type coins than the uni-cephalic Chitreśvara type described above. The two types are, however, linked together by their legend and devices though the form of Śiva on them changes from tri-cephalic to uni-cephalic.

Shastri had rightly observed that "These coins are of great interest to a student of early Indian iconography and religious history" as the earliest similar representation of Śiva from Gudimallam shows the uni-cephalous god in a standing posture on the shoulders of Apasmāra-purusha whereas on the coins under discussion, the three-headed god is depicted as seated with his legs resting on the body, not shoulders, of the kneeling figure, and "Our coins, thus, afford us the oldest depiction of the *Apasmāra-purusha* in the North, and the earliest seated representation in the Indian subcontinent". Drawing attention to the depiction of Poseidon holding a trident on the coins of Antimachus I Theos and the same deity on some copper coins of Maues standing with right foot resting on a small radiant figure underneath him Shastri observes that "Trident and the figure underneath are two points common to these representations of Poseidon and the *apasmāra-purusha*. Whether the former played any role in the development of the concept and visual representation of the latter cannot be ascertained at the moment; but some such possibility cannot altogether be ruled out, particularly in view of the chronological and spatial proximity between these Indo-Scythian coins and the Kuṇinda pieces in question" (Shastri

1984: p. 31). The Greeks, Scythians and Parthians generally represented the king on the obverse and some deity on the reverse of their coins. Indo-Greek (especially those of Apollodotus), Kuṇinda and Audumbara coins are often found together (O.C. Handa 1984: pp. 132-139). The Kuṇinda coins were struck on the pattern of alien coins with whom they seem to have trade, so the influence was likely and natural. Contrarily many of the republican states of ancient India seem to have given more importance to their gods than their rulers and represented the deities or their symbols on the obverse and the symbols representing the rulers on the reverse. The coins under discussion represent single or three-headed Śiva on the obverse and symbolical representation of the ruling authority on the reverse. The large number of varieties of these coins indicate a long span of circulation coeval with hex-cephalic Kārttikeya/Shashṭhī and Kārttikeya/Deer type Yaudheya coins.

4

Provenience, Date and Attribution

Coins of Chitreśvara type were quite rare and only a few other pieces were known till a few decades back. All the coins of known provenance come from Garhwal-Kumaon or the adjoining plains only. Rapson had noted 'the influence of the large copper money of the Kuṣāṇas' on the (uni-cephalous) Chitreśvara type coins and assigned them to the third or fourth century CE (Rapson 1897: p. 12). Allan, too, placed them about three centuries later than the Amoghabhūti type (Allan 1936: p. ci). All subsequent writers have also recognized a gap of about two or three centuries in the Amoghabhūti and Chitreśvara types which, as noted above, were attributed to the Kuṇindas by Cunningham. Though some scholars have pointed out the similarities between the Brahmaṇyadeva and Chitreśvara types (Powell-Price 1945: pp. 214 ff; Singh and Ahmad 1977: p. 63; Shastri 1987: p. 29) yet most of the scholars like Rapson (1897: p. 12, Pl. III.9-10), Smith (1906: pp. 161 & 167-70), Allan (1936: pp. ciii & 152-68), Chakrabortty (1935-36: pp. 75-77), M.K. Sharan (1972: pp. 282 ff), Bela Lahiri (1974: pp. 233 ff), Dasgupta (1974: pp. 90-94), Mitchiner (1976: pp. 632-35), Shastri (1984: p. 28), P.L. Gupta (1988: pp. 24-26), Richard Mann (2007: pp. 65-66), Sircar (1968b: p. 213), etc. have accepted this attribution as final. The contemporaneity of Brahmaṇyadeva and Chitreśvara types is evident even in the Garhwal Hoard. More than a hundred varieties listed above indicate a large expanse of time span for them which is revealed even by their palaeography.

Recently Sushmita Basu Majumdar (2019: 103) has come out with a new identification of these coins regarding them to be the joint issues of the Yaudheyas and Kuṇindas "as the Kuṇinda motifs (deer, *svastika*, etc.) are very much distinct on this category of coins. It may also be pointed out here that the deity on the Kuṇinda coins has been placed beside the Yaudheya deity on another type of coins which reflects equal status of both the clans and thus on this ground these issues may be considered as joint issues of the Yaudheyas and Kuṇindas." In the very next sentence, however, she almost contradicts herself by saying that "The reason behind the issuance of this joint coinage was a monetary alliance or a political alliance between the Yaudheyas and Kuṇindas is (sic.) not very clear due to dearth of evidence." She then puts a wrong statement that "D. Handa however attributes these issues to a tribe (clan) named Kāḍa and identifies Sugh as their residing place" (*Ibid.*). I regard Kāḍa coins as different from Kuṇinda coins though both types have been found from Sugh (Handa 2006: pp. 72-85 & 99-114). Another argument put forth by her regarding the Chitreśvara type coins is that "neither does it bear the name of the Yaudheyas nor does it bear the name of the Kuṇindas. Hence this should be regarded as a joint issue of both as suggested above." She continues to state that "Even in that case Yaudheya influence is stronger as the obverse bears the legend or the name of the deity and the reverse is uninscribed" (Majumdar 2019: p. 104). The alliance between the Yaudheyas and the Kuṇindas is unsubstantiated by facts. Referring to the Yaudheya coins of mono-cephalous Kārttikeya-Devasenā type bearing the figure of single-headed Kārttikeya with peacock near his left foot and the legend 'Yaudheya-gaṇasya jaya' around on the obverse and his spouse Devasenā on the reverse and the crudeness of Chitreśvara type coins Sushmita Basu Majumdar has made another preposterous statement that "The figure had undergone a process of degeneration to this extent that the die cutter could not imagine it as a peacock and turned it into a human figure kneeling down with bowed head touching the ground like *apasmāra-puruṣa*" (*Ibid*). It may be pointed out that Kārttikeya-Devasenā type coins are posterior to tri-cephalic Chitreśvara type coins and could not have served as model for the latter. A comparison of the two types would clearly betray the hollowness of this argument –

Comparison between Kārttikeya-Devasenā type coins and Chitreśvara type coins

The geographical distribution of the Amoghabhūti and Chitreśvara types is very significant. The former circulated in a very vast area extending from Kangra-Mandi in Himachal Pradesh to Almora-Kashipur in Uttarakhand and the adjoining plains of Punjab, Haryana and western Uttar Pradesh while the latter was confined to Garhwal.

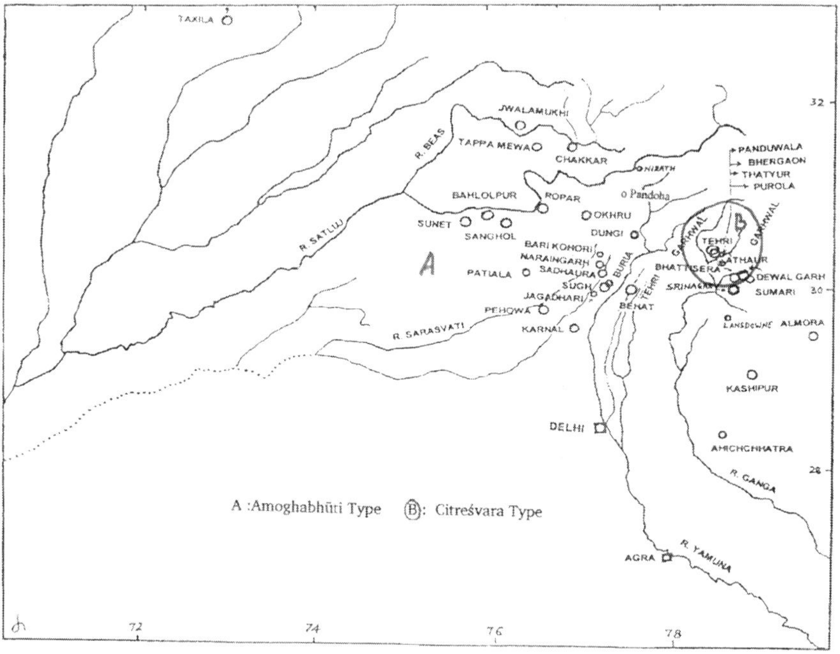

The Kuṇindas: The Distribution of their Coins

It is also notable that no hoard of Amoghabhūti type coins has ever yielded any Chitreśvara type coins nor have the latter been definitely known to be found from any place besides the Garhwal-Kumaon hills and the adjoining plains of western Uttar Pradesh. Thus not only the provenances of the two types are distinct, the evidence of all the Kuṇinda coin-hoards also goes against putting them together. On the other hand, the Garhwal hoard consisting only of the above-mentioned Chitreśvara type and Shaḍānana-Deer type Yaudheya coins and one Chitreśvara type coin with thirteen Shaḍānana-Deer type coins from Tehri-Garhwal published sometime back indicate that Chitreśvara and Shaḍānana (Brahmaṇyadeva) types should go together. It is well known that being pressed by alien incursions the Yaudheyas found safer resort in the Garhwal hills where they struck coins in the name of their tutelary god hex-cephalic Kārttikeya bearing the legend *Bhagavata svāmino Brahmaṇyadevasya Kumārasya* or allied versions. The distribution map of Yaudheya coins of this type bears it out very clearly.

Both these types show a great affinity of fabric, execution, motifs and even legends.

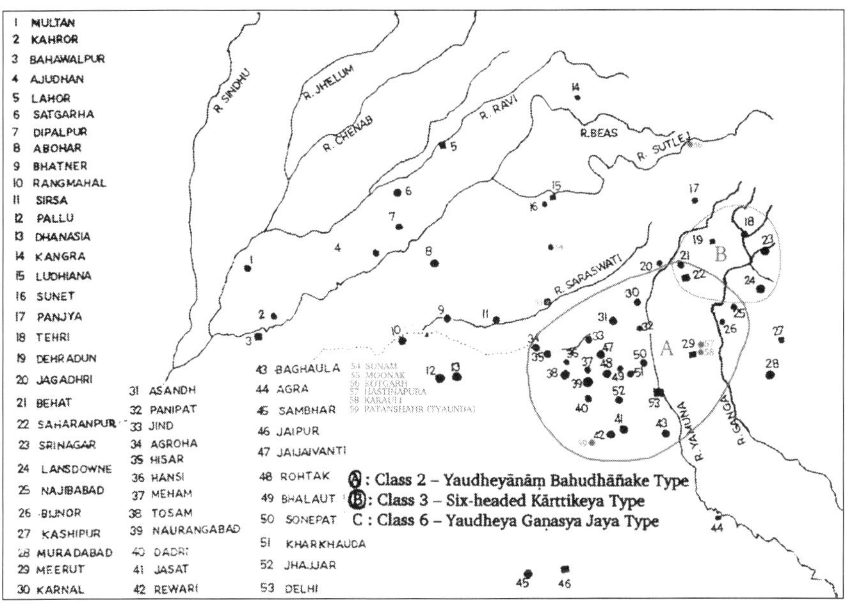

Map showing the distribution of main types of Yaudheya and Chitreśvara type coins

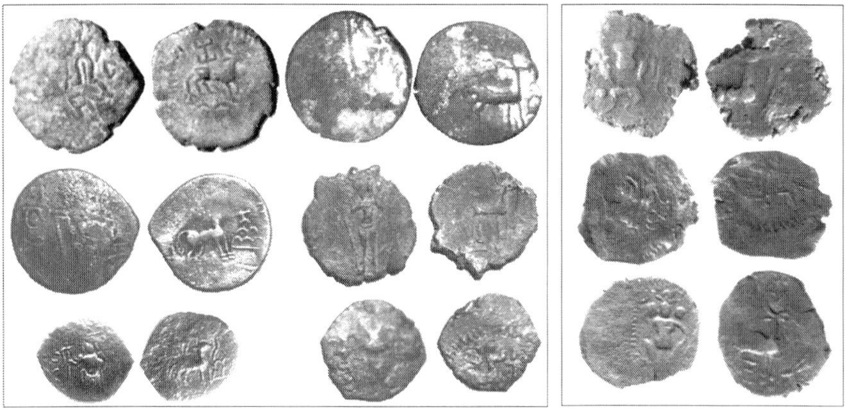

Comparable fabric of Yaudheya and Chitreśvara type coins

Prof. Shastri had observed that the Chitreśvara type coins "bear such a close resemblance to the Yaudheya specie of Allan's class III, particularly in regard to reverse devices, that one could as well be tempted to ascribe them to the Yaudheyas". However, while publishing the tricephalic Chitreśvara coins, Prof. Shastri observed that they provide, for the first time, "unimpeachable evidence in support of their attribution to the Kuṇindas" even though none of these coins bears the name of Amoghabhūti. Referring to the extremely close affinity, verging on identity, between the obverse composition of Amoghabhūti coins and the reverse of the tri-cephalous Śiva-Chitreśvara coin nos. 1 and 2 of the Garhwal Hoard published by him, he held that "the latter may be justifiably regarded as the immediate successors of the former" and concluded that "The seated Śiva type, therefore, affords a hitherto missing link, both typological and chronological, between the Amoghabhūti and so far doubtfully ascribed Kuṇinda specie", i.e. uni-cephalous Śiva-Chitreśvara type coins. Relying on the reverse device of these coins which are almost exactly identical with those of the obverse of Amoghabhūti's coins, Shastri feels that the seated Śiva type coins afford a hitherto missing link, both typological and chronological, between the Amoghabhūti and so far doubtfully ascribed Chitreśvara type Kuṇinda specie (Shastri 1984: 28). The execution, fabric, etc. of the three-headed Śiva type coins is the sure evidence of their being earlier than the uni-cephalic Chitreśvara coins. Their circulation along with the hex-cephalic

Kārttikeya type coins which are definitely earlier than the uni-cephalous Chitreśvara type coins struck on the Kushāṇa module and showing much better execution also corroborates it. M.P. Joshi (1989: pp. 141-45) assigns the tri-cephalic Chitreśvara type to a later date than the uni-cephalic one but we have already discussed above the reasons for the priority of the former on the latter and the tri-cephalic type being the immediate successors of Amoghabhūti type coins. Explaining the cause of the change of type, Shastri (Shastri 1984: p. 28) observed that "when the Kuṇindas decided to depict Śiva on the obverse of their coins, they relegated the obverse devices of Amoghabhūti specie to the reverse" and cited the example of Nahapāna who relegated the obverse devices of the copper coins of Bhūmaka to the reverse of his bust type silver coinage. But one may ask as to what was the expediency for the Kuṇindas to change the type? And that too in a very limited area of Garhwal whereas their copper coins of coarse fabric of Amoghabhūti type, which are almost of the same period, were circulating in a much wider area. Were the Kuṇindas too squeezed to this area by the Kushāṇas and like the Yaudheyas dedicated their state to their tutelary deity? Firstly, there is no definite evidence of the Kushāṇas having pressed the Kuṇindas so hard and squeezed them to this limited area; secondly, though the Kuṇindas may have been worshipping Śiva, it cannot be said with any amount of certainty that Śiva-Chitreśvara was their tutelary deity. God Chitreśvara was probably popularly worshipped in Garhwal-Kumaon region whereas Śiva was worshipped in a very large area in the hills. Even if for the sake of argument we accept that these Chitreśvara type coins were issued by the Kuṇindas how shall we explain the circulation of Shaḍānana-Brahmaṇyadeva type coins in the same region and at the same time? In Indian numismatics, however, the continuation and/or adoption of a popular motif or device by a succeeding or conqueror dynasty have not been an uncommon feature. Silver coins of Apollodotus and the so-called Mahādeva type show bull and elephant as the main devices on the two sides. These very devices are found on the copper square coins of Heliocles (Gardner 1966: Pl. VII.6), Maues (*Ibid*, Pl. XVII.6), and Vemaka coins (Allan 1936: p. 280, Pl. VII.6). Elephant head and caduceus are found on the obverse and reverse of the copper round coins of Demetrius and Maues

(Gardner 1966: Pls. III.2 & XVI respectively). After conquering Gujarat, Chandragupta II started issuing Western Kshatrapa type silver coins. Some post-Gupta rulers of Bengal adopted the reverse motifs of the Guptas. The Bull / Horseman devices of the Hindu Shāhis were adopted by the Chāhamānas, Gāhaḍavālas and even the Turks. Similarly, the seated Lakshmī device initiated by king Gāṅgeyedeva of the Kalachuri dynasty of Tripurī is to be found on the coins of the Chandelas, Chāhamānas, Tomaras, Gāhaḍavālas as well as the Turks. So the adoption of a device, we think, does not necessarily mean the continuation of a dynasty that had initially made use of it. The module of the Chitreśvara type coins is closer to the Shaḍānana-Brahmaṇyadeva type coins than Amoghabhūti's coins. Chronologically the uni-cephalic Chitreśvara type coins were issued about three centuries later than the Amoghabhūti type coins. Amoghabhūti issued bimetallic currency whereas Chitreśvara coins are available only in copper. Amoghabhūti issued biscriptual coins but Chitreśvara coins show only Brāhmī legends which too are very fragmentary like the legends of the Shaḍānana-Brahmaṇyadeva type coins. Amoghabhūti's coins are quite copious in silver are comparatively rare in copper but Chitreśvara type coins, though considered quite rare before the discovery of Garhwal Hoard, are now known in more than hundred varieties as listed above. The Brāhmī legend on the silver and copper coins of Amoghabhūti invariably begins from near 9 o'clock position whereas the legend on Chitreśvara type coins generally begins from near 1–2 o'clock position and shows variations like Shaḍānana-Brahmaṇyadeva type and *Yaudheya-gaṇasya-jaya* type coins of the Yaudheyas.

The Kuṇinda coins show deer facing Lakshmī on the obverse. This identification of the goddess has been accepted by all scholars. The Chitreśvara type coins betray the allegiance of their issuers to Śiva. Why did they substitute worship of Lakshmī by that of Śiva and what was the rationale behind it has not been explained by any scholar. The Yaudheyas worshipping Śiva and depicting him on their coins on the other hand is very logical.

We do not hear of the Kuṇindas in the Allahabad *Praśasti* probably because they had ceased to exist as a political entity much before that. The Yaudheyas, being hard-pressed by the Śakas and the Kushāṇas, were forced to seek refuge in the hilly region of the Western Himalayas. They may have occupied this region after the Kuṇinda power dwindled in the area. Long back, P.L. Gupta (1950: p. 173) had concluded that the Yaudheyas occupied a considerable portion of the tract around Dehradun, which was once under the occupation of the Kuṇindas. M.C. Joshi (1960: p. 30) had suggested long ago that the Chitreśvara type coins were "issued by the composite people consisting of native (Kuṇindas) and migrated (Yaudheya) elements". Since the worship of Śiva had a very long and strong tradition in this area, the Yaudheyas seem to have issued coins in the name of Chitreśvara, in addition to the Brahmaṇyadeva/Deer type coins. Some Brahmaṇyadeva type coins also show Śiva with trident (Allan 1936: p. 275, no. 79, Pl. XL.13; Singh and Ahmad 1977, 171). Even Kārttikeya holding a trident in his right or left hand instead of the usual lance, has been noticed on some coins of the Garhwal Hoard (Handa 2007: Pl. XLIX.1-2).

Trident bearing deities on Garhwal Hoard coins

The Garhwal Hoard contains a coin (Negative no. 380/1-6, card no. 150) where six-headed Kārttikeya too is shown as holding the trident in his right hand and sitting just like the tri-cephalous Śiva-Chitreśvara –

Some Yaudheya coins of this hoard show inverted tree symbol at the back of the deer like the ones of tri-cephalous Śiva-Chitreśvara type (Negative no. 380/3-6, card no. 197) –

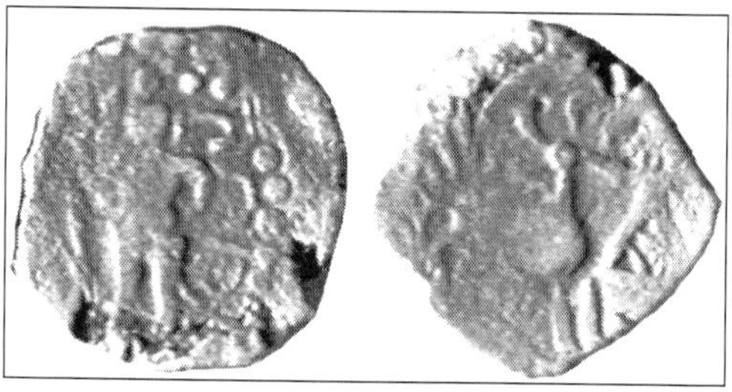

The deer facing a temple surmounted by a trident on the reverse corroborates Śiva worship by the Yaudheyas in the Garhwal region. Subsidiary symbols like the triangle-headed staff, *śrīvatsa*, vase, *svastika*, etc. on the back of the deer on the reverse too are seen on some Yaudheya coins in this hoard (Negative no. 379/3-18, card no. 138) –

Deer facing arched symbol with water-channel flowing from its base is also common to the Yaudheya and Śiva-Chitreśvara types.

Sometimes it becomes very difficult even to distinguish the two series when we have crudely executed and worn out pieces.

The earliest Yaudheya coins of 'Yaudheyānāṃ Bahudhāñake' type show bull device and their clay sealings usually depict bull as the prominent device indicating that they were worshippers of Śiva. They may have worshipped Śiva as a great deity (Mahādeva) and father of Kārttikeya.

Yaudheya sealings with bull device

Though the Yaudheyas dedicated their state to their tutelary deity, the divine War-God Kārttikeya, when they shifted to the Garhwal region under alien pressure and struck coins in his name, they continued to worship Śiva and issued coins depicting the god as noted above. Some of their Kārttikeya/Deer type coins show the deer facing a temple with trident atop indicating their continued worship of Śiva –

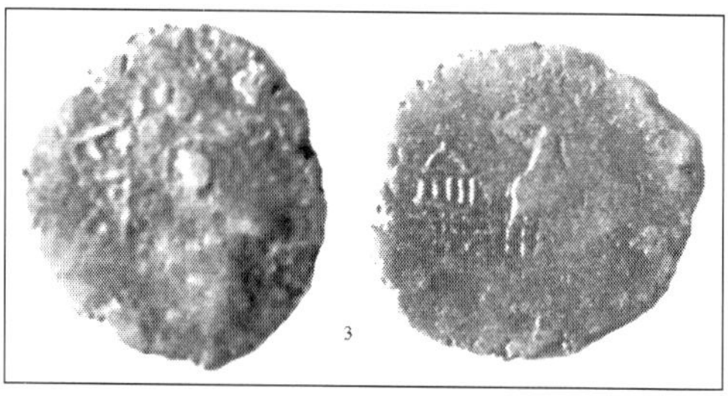

So the striking of Śiva-Chitreśvara coins by the Yaudheyas should not surprise us at all. The standing posture, the dress, the left hand on hip and the stance of the right hand of Śiva and Kārttikeya on the unicephalous Chitreśvara and Yaudheya coins compares very favourably with each other. The legends too are comparable. The retrograde legend on some Chitreśvara type coins is comparable to similar retrograde legends on Kārttikeye/Deer type Yaudheya coins:

Chitreśvara and Brahmaṇyadeva type coins with retrograde legends

The foregoing discussion, thus, makes it amply clear that the Chitreśvara type coins are distinct from Amoghabhūti type coins of the Kuṇindas and should go together with the Brahmaṇyadeva type coins of the Yaudheyas with which they betray similarities of fabric, execution, motifs, legend and its disposition, provenance and chronology.

The following points summarized from the above discussion are, therefore, worth consideration in this connection –

1. Chitreśvara types are localized to Garhwal and adjoining region only.
2. No hoard of Amoghabhūti type coins has ever yielded any Chitreśvara type coins.
3. Chitreśvara and Brahmaṇyadeva type coins have often been found together.
4. Chitreśvara and Brahmaṇyadeva types betray similarities of fabric, execution, motifs, legends and even their disposition.
5. As noted above Prof. Shastri had rightly observed that Chitreśvara type coins "bear such a close resemblance to the Yaudheya specie of Allan's Class III, particularly in regard to reverse devices, that one could as well be tempted to ascribe them to the Yaudheyas."
6. Chitreśvara type coins are very scarce as compared to the copious currency of Amoghabhūti.
7. Amoghabhūti type is available in silver as well as copper whereas Chitreśvara coins are confined only to copper like the Brahmanyadeva type coins.
8. Amoghabhūti issued biscriptual coins while Chitreśvara types are unilingual.
9. Brahmaṇyadeva coins have varieties showing Śiva and Kārttikeya holding the trident.
10. In mythology, Chitreśvara (Śiva) is the father of Kārttikeya (Brahmaṇyadeva).
11. The inclination towards Śiva worship by the Yaudheyas is indicated by their earliest coins and seals and sealings which depict humped bull.
12. The Kuṇinda coins show deer facing Lakshmī on the obverse indicating their allegiance to the goddess but Chitreśvara type coins betray Śaiva worship for which there is no explanation and rationale.
13. The provenance of both the Brahmaṇyadeva and Chitreśvara type coins is the same.
14. Like the transition of six-headed Kārttikeya on Shaḍānana-Deer (Brahmaṇyadeva) type to single-headed Kārttikeya on Kārttikeya-Devasenā type the Chitreśvara type coins also show the change from tri-cephalous to uni-cephalous type of Śiva.

15. The obverse and reverse devices on the coins of the two series run almost parallel on certain varieties with the only difference of the deity and legend.
16. The crude and careless workmanship of Shaḍānana-Deer and tri-cephalous Śiva-Chitreśvara type coins (which are often found together) is similar.
17. On both series the arched *chaitya* is sometimes shown with a line flowing from its base.
18. The period of currency of these two types is also the same.

We, therefore, feel inclined to regard Chitreśvara type coins to have been issued by the Yaudheyas (Handa 1999: pp. 33-43). This, however, poses a difficulty as these coins too like the Brahmaṇyadeva coins (Types III and IV) are dedicatory in nature. How could the Yaudheya dedicate their state to both Śiva and Kārttikeya? It is well known that Kārttikeya, the tutelary deity of the Yaudheyas, is the son of Śiva. The depiction of bull on the Bull-Elephant or Bahudhānyaka type and of Śiva on the Brahmaṇya type coins has been taken generally as indicative of their Śaivite leanings (Singh and Ahmad 1977: pp. 89-90 & 130-31). When under the alien pressure the Yaudheyas were obliged to find safer refuge in the hills of Tehri-Garhwal where they probably found a strong tradition of Śiva worship and dedicated their state to their tutelary deity as well as to Śiva-Chitreśvara, the sire of their generalissimo, whose worship was very popular in the area occupied by them. That a quasi-theocracy practising administration of a realm in the name of a divinity or divinities was not unusual in early times is revealed by an analogous instance of the illustrious king Gautamīputra Vṛishadhvaja who made over his kingdom to 'Maheśvara-Mahāsena' as known from a seal of *circa* third-fourth century CE discovered from Bhita in Uttar Pradesh – *'Śrī-Vindhya-bhedana-mahārājasya Maheśvara-Mahāsenātisṛishṛa-rājyasya Vṛishadhvajasya Gautamīputrasya'* (*ASIAR* 1911-12: p. 51). Elsewhere I have shown that the Yaudheyas worshipped not only Śiva and Kārttikeya but also various other gods to which they dedicated shrines depicted on their Kārttikeya-Deer type coins (Handa 2007: pp. 190-98). Another point worthy of note here is the identity of Śiva with various gods including Skanda as described in his Viśvarūpa in the *Liṅgapurāṇa* (Part II, Chapter XVIIII, vv. 1-4):

Ya esha bhagavān Rudra Brahmā-Vishṇu-Maheśvaraḥ /
Skandaśchāpi tathā Chandro bhuvanāni chaturdaśa //

. . . .

. . . .

. . . .

. . . .

Tvamādi cha tathābhūto bhūrbhavaḥ svastathaiva cha /
Aute tvaṃ viśvarūpo'si śīshantu jagataḥ sadā //

My attribution of Chitreśvara type coins to the Yaudheyas was endorsed by Amiteshwar Jha (2003: 35). It is gratifying to note that Wilfried Pieper who subscribed to the Kuṇinda attribution of Chitreśvara type coins earlier (Pieper 2013: p. 378) has also accepted my attribution of these coins to the Yaudheyas. He observes that "Whereas earlier I have shared the Kuṇinda attribution, now I think Handa's Yaudheya attribution has the greater merit. It is also more compatible with the typological continuation of the coin types in question and as for the female deity on the seated Śiva type a Pārvatī identification makes more sense than to regard her as Lakṣmī" (Pieper 2015: pp. 50-51. See also Pieper 2021: p. 251).

Bibliography

Allan, John (1936), *Catalogue of the Coins of Ancient India*, British Museum, London, (reprint, Munshiram Manoharlal, New Delhi, 1975).

Altekar, A.S. (1954), in *Vākāṭaka-Gupta Age*, 2nd edn, (Eds. R.C. Majumdar and A.S. Altekar), Banaras.

Archaeological Survey of India, Annual Report, 1911-12.

Bajpai, K.D. (1973), 'Yaudheya Coins – A Critical Study', *JNSI*, XXXV.

Banerjea, J.N. (1951), 'The reading and interpretation of some Yaudheya coin legends', *Journal of the Numismatic Society of India*, XIII (II), pp. 160-63.

Banerjea, J.N. (1956), *Development of Hindu Icononography*, 2nd edn, Calcutta.

Banerjea, J.N. (1957), in *Comprehensive History of India*, Vol. II (edited by K.A.N. Sastri).

Chakrabortty, S.K. (1931), *Studies in Ancient Indian Numismatics*, Mymensingh.

Chakrabortty, S.K. (1935-36), 'The Tribal Coins of Northern India', *Numismatic Supplement*, No. XLVI, pp. 75-77.

Chattopadhyay, Sudhakar (1958), *Early History of North India*, Calcutta.

Cunningham, Alexander, *Archaeological Survey Report*, Vol. XIV.

Cunningham, Alexander (1891), *Coins of Ancient India*, London (Reprint, Varanasi, 1963).

Dasgupta, K.K. (1974), *Tribal History of Ancient India - A Numismatic Approach*, Calcutta.

Dayal, P. (1940), 'A New Hoard of Yaudheya Coins from Dehra Dun District', *Journal of the Numismatic Society of India*, III, pp. 109-12.

Face Book/Internet/Trade

Gupta, L.C. (1985), 'Some Copper Coins from Tehri Garhwal', *JNSI*, XLVII, pp. 14-17.

Gupta, L.C. (1986), 'Some Rare Kuninda Coins', *JNSI*, XLVIII, pp. 36-40.

Gupta, P.L. (1950), 'The Yaudheyas', *Journal of the U.P. Historical Society*, Vol. XXIII, pp. 169-174.

Gupta, P.L. (1987), 'The Brahmanya coins', *Numismatic Digest*, Vol. XI, pp. 28-39.

Gupta, P.L. (1988), *Numismatic History of Himachal Pradesh Pradesh and the Catalogue of Coins in Himachal State Museum, Shimla and Bhuri Singh Museum, Chamba*, Delhi: B.R. Publications.

Handa, Devendra (1991), 'The Yaudheyas and Their Coins', Numismatic Studies, Vol. I.

Handa, Devendra (1994), *Numismatic Digest*, 18, pp. 25-26.

Handa, Devendra (1996), 'Three-Headed Śiva-Chitreśvara Type Copper Coins,' *Oriental Numismatic Studies*, Vol. 1, New Delhi: Harman Publishing House, pp. 81-85, Pls. I.3-8 and II.1-3.

Handa, Devendra (1999), 'The Attribution of Chitreśvara Type Coins,' *Oriental Numismatic Studies*, Vol. 2, New Delhi, pp. 33-43.

Handa, Devendra (July 2001), *IIRNS Newsline*, Issue 31, p. 5.

Handa, Devendra (2006), *Early Indian Coins from Sugh*, New Delhi: Sundeep Prakashan.

Handa, Devendra (2007), *Tribal Coins of Ancient India*, New Delhi: Aryan Books International.

Handa, O.C. (1984), Numismatic *Sources on the Early History of Western Himalaya*, Delhi: B.R. Publishing.

Jha, Amiteshwar (2003), *Bhāratīya Sikke Eka Aitihāsika Parichaya*, Anjaneri (Nasik): IIRNS (revised edition 2013).

Joshi, M.C. (1960), 'Kuṇinda Coinage: A Review', *Bhāratīya Vidyā*, Vol. XXII.

Joshi, M.P. (1989), *Morphogenesis of the Kuṇindas – A Numismatic Overview*, Almora.

Kala, S.C. (1946), 'Further Light on the Territories of the Kunindas', *JNSI*, VIII, pp. 36-38.

Kala, S.C. (1956), 'Some Interesting Coins of the Yaudheyas', *JNSI*, XVIII, pp. 46-48.

Kumar, Manmohan (1996), 'Ancient Mint at Rohtak', in *Numismatic Panorama: Essays in Memory of Late Shri S. M. Shukla*, eds. K.K. Maheshwari and B. Rath, New Delhi: Harman.

Lahiri, Bela (1974), *Indigenous States of Northern India*, Calcutta.

Mahābhārata (Ray's edition)

Majumdar, R.C. (Ed.), *Age of Imperial Unity*, 4th edn, Bombay, 1968.

Majumdar, Sushmita Basu (2019), 'Kuninda Coins in the British Museum Collection: A Critical Analysis' in *Money and Monetary Matters in Pre-modern South Asia*, edited by Sushmita Basu Majumdar & S.K. Bose, New Delhi: Manohar.

Mann, Richard D. (2007). 'Yaudheya Chronology and Coinage: An Analysis', *Numismatic Digest*, Vol. 31, pp. 47-113.

Marudhar Arts, e-Auction 30

Mitchiner, Michael (1976), *Indo-Greek and Indo-Scythian Coins*, Vol. 7, London: Hawkins.

Pieper, Wilfried (2013), *Ancient Indian Coins Revisited*, Lancaster/London: Classical Numismatic Group Inc.

Pieper, Wilfried (2015), 'The Earliest Saivite Images on Ancient Indian Coins', *Numismatic Digest*, Vol. 39, pp. 27-84.

Pieper, Wilfried (2021), *Ancient Indian Coins: A Comprehensive Catalogue*, Anjaneri/Mumbai: IIRNS Publications.

Powell-Price, J.C. (July-Dec. 1945), 'Kunindas and Katyuras', *Journal of the U.P. Historical Society*, XVIII (i-ii), pp. 214 ff.

Prakash, Jai (1965), 'Observations on the Tribal Coinages of Ancient India', *JNSI*, XXVII, pp. 123-141.

Prinsep, James (1858), *Essays in Indian Antiquities* (edited by E. Thomas), London.

Rapson, E.J. (1897), *Indian Coins*, Strassburg.

Ray, Himanshu Prabha (Ed.) (2010), *Sanghol and the Archaeology of Punjab*, New Delhi: Aryan Books International.

Sastri, K.A.N. (Ed), *Comprehensive History of India*, Vol. II, Bombay-Calcutta-Madras, 1957.

Sharan, M.K. (1972), *Tribal Coins – A Study*, New Delhi.

Shastri, Ajay Mitra (1984), 'Interesting Kuninda and Yaudheya Coins,' *Numismatic Digest (ND)*, VIII, pp. 24-34.

Shastri, Ajaya Mitra (1987), 'Some Observations on the 'Mandi' Hoard of Yaudheya and Kuninda Coins', *Numismatic Digest*, XI.

Singh, Jai Prakash and Nisar Ahmad (Ed.) (1977), *Seminar Papers on the Tribal Coins of Ancient India (c. 200 B.C. to 400 A.D.)*, Varanasi: NSI.

Sircar, D.C. (1968a), in *The Age of Imperial Unity*, 4th edn, Bombay (edited by R.C. Majumdar and A.D. Pusalkar, Bombay).

Sircar, D.C. (1968b), *Studies in Indian Coins*, Delhi: MLBD.

Wikipedia

Zeno.ru

Index

Aggarwal, R.K. (collection) 17, 18
Ahmad, Nisar 70, 77, 82
Allahabad *Praśasti* 76
Allan, John 2, 4-5, 7-9, 11, 13, 65, 70, 74, 77, 80
Almora 4, 72, 77
Altekar, A.S. 2

Amoghabhūti 3, 6, 8, 65-67, 70, 72-73, 75-76, 80-81
Antimachus I Theos 68
Apollodotus 69, 75
Audumbara 69

BACRI/hoard 6, 7, 59
Banerjea, J.N. 2, 4
Behat 1, 5, 6
Bengal 76
Bhita 82
Bhūmaka 75
British Museum 4-6, 8-15, 35-36, 59-61

Chāhamānas 76
Chakrabortty, S.K. 3, 70
Chandelas 76
Chandragupta II 76
Chitreshwar Śiva Temple 4
Cunningham, Alexander 1-3, 5-6, 8, 66, 70

Dasgupta, K.K. 2, 4-5, 11, 13, 70
Dehradun 7, 77
Demetrius 75

Gāhaḍavālas 76
Gaṅgā 60
Gāṅgeyadeva 76
Gautamīputra Vṛishadhvaja 82
Gopeshwar 3
Gudimallam 68
Gujarat 76
Gupta, L.C. 5, 7
Gupta, P.L. 5-8, 70, 77
Gurukula Museum 23

Haryana 6, 72
Heliocles 75
Himachal Pradesh 72
Hindu Shāhis 76

INHCRF (collection) 6, 29, 39, 41-44, 46-47, 52-53, 58, 61-63
Iyer, Venki (collection) 33

Jain, Akshay (collection) 11, 22
Jha, Amiteshwar 83
Jharkhand 4
Joshi, M.C. 3, 77
Joshi, M.P. 75

Kāḍa coins 71
Kalachuri 76
Kala, S.C. 6, 7
Kangra 72
Karnal 6
Kashipur 72
Keśarī dynasty 4
Kuṇinda/s 1, 2, 3, 5, 6, 8, 65, 66, 68, 70, 71, 73-77, 80-81, 83
Kushān/Kushāṇa 3, 75-76

Lahiri, Bela 70
Lakshmī 66, 76, 81, 83
Lansdowne 7
Liṅgapurāṇa 82
Lingen, Jan (collection) 5, 15, 67

Mahābhārata 4
Maheshwari, K.K. (collection) 6, 36-37, 42-43, 47, 51, 63
Majumdar, Sushmita Basu 71
Mandi 6, 72
Mann, Richard 70
Marudhar Arts 19, 33
Maues 68, 75
Mitra, R.L. 6
Mitchner, Michael 16, 70

Nahapāna 75
National Museum 20

Odisha 4

Panjya 7
Parekh, Hardik (collection) 16
Pārvatī 68, 83
Pieper, Wilfried 19, 61, 83
Poseidon 68
Powell-Price 70
Prinsep, James 1, 5-6
Punjab 3, 72

Rapson 70
Ray, Himanshu Prabha 20

Saharanpur 1
Śaka 3, 76
Sharan, M.K. 70
Shastri, Ajay Mitra 2, 4, 6-8, 33-35, 43-45, 60, 68, 70, 74-75, 81
Singh, Jai Prakash 3, 70, 77, 82
Singh, Karan (collection) 16, 19
Sircar, D.C. 3, 70
Skandapurāṇa 4
Smith 70
Somavaṃśī dynasty 4
Srinagar 6
Sugh 71
Sunet 6
Suvarṇarekhā 4

Tomaras 76
Tripuri 76
Turks 76
Tye, Robert & Monica 6, 36, 59, 61

Udeshi, Amit (collection) 22
Uttarakhand 4, 6-7, 72
Uttar Pradesh 6, 72-73, 82

Vemaka 75

Yaudheya/s 1, 7-8, 65-67, 69, 71, 73-83